A PEANUTS HALLOWEEN

TRICK OR TREAT!

CHARLES M. SCHULZ

BALLANTINE BOOKS • NEW YORK

A Ballantine Book
Published by The Random House Publishing Group

Copyright © 2004 United Feature Syndicate, Inc.
Foreword copyright © 2004 by R. L. Stine

www.ballantinebooks.com
www.snoopy.com

Grateful acknowledgement is made to the following for permission to print previously published material:
Recipes on pages 42 and 106 from *The Pillsbury Complete Cookbook* by The Pillsbury Company, copyright © 2000 by the Pillsbury Company.
Used by permission of Clarkson Potter Publishers, a division of Random House, Inc.
Recipe on page 77 provided by Allrecipes.com, the world's favorite recipe site. Peppermint Patty Brownies recipe submitted by Pam.
Recipe on page 9 provided by Allrecipes.com, the world's favorite recipe site. Caramel Apples recipe submitted by Suzie.
Crafts on pages 22, 29, 32, 101, and recipes on pages 74 and 107 from *Halloween Treats* copyright © 1998 by Donna Maggipinto.
Used by permission of Chronicle Books LLC, San Francisco. Visit Chroniclebooks.com.

Library of Congress Control Number: 2004093799

ISBN 0-345-46413-3

Cover design by United Media

Manufactured in the United States of America

First Edition: October 2004

2 4 6 8 9 7 5 3 1

Design by Diane Hobbing of Snap-Haus Graphics

TRICK OR TREAT!

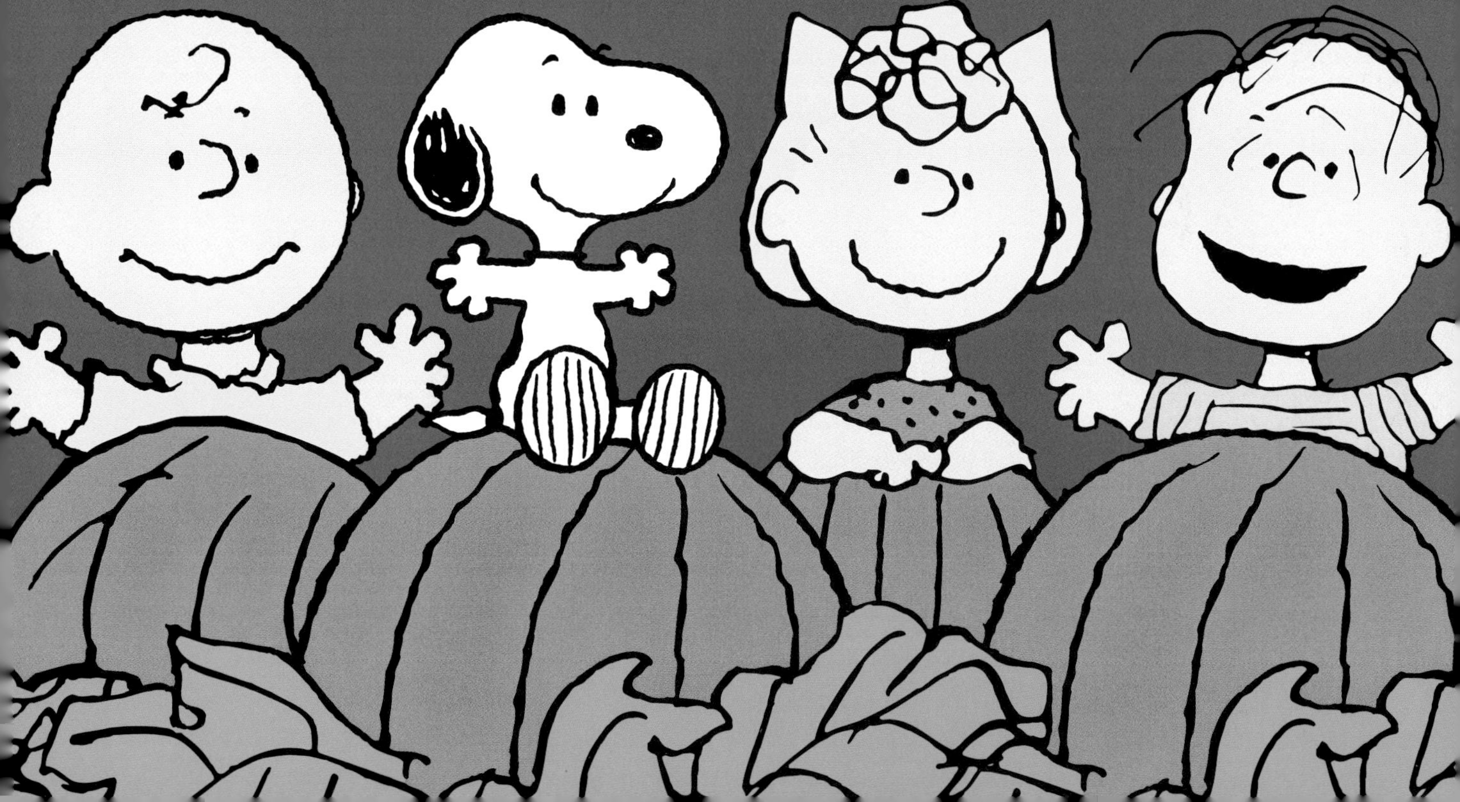

When doing the recipes or crafts, children should be accompanied by an adult.

Foreword

I've been reading *Peanuts* practically my entire life, but Halloween has always been my favorite time to read about Charlie Brown and his friends. Watching the full moon rise over Linus's pumpkin patch every October was always funny and poignant and shivery at the same time.

My scariest Halloween happened when I was about Charlie Brown's age, and it still gives me chills every time I think about it.

My brother Bill and I were excited because that year we were allowed to go trick-or-treating by ourselves. No parents. We were dressed as ghosts, with eyeholes cut into bedsheets. We both carried shopping bags to hold our treats. And in case a little *tricking* was called for, I slipped an aerosol can of liquid cobwebs (you know, that stringy stuff) under my costume.

We stepped out into a cold October night. A strong breeze made the bare trees shiver. The ground was crunchy hard and shiny with frost. A sliver of a moon beamed down on us like a tilted smile.

At the bottom of the driveway, I gazed at Mrs. Dawson's house across the street. No porch light on. The windows were all dark. "She's not home," I told my brother.

We started toward the next house and went up the block, running from one side of the street to the other. It felt good to be ghosts, floating through the neighborhood wild and free, our sheets flapping behind us as we ran.

The houses were close together, so we made a lot of stops. By the time we returned home an hour later, our shopping bags were bulging with candy.

Once again I turned to Mrs. Dawson's house. This time, I saw an orange glow in the front window. I squinted hard and saw a grinning jack-o'-lantern face. Two tiny triangle eyes and a jagged, yellow-orange smile floated in the dark window.

"She's home," I said. "Let's go."

A few seconds later, we rang her doorbell. We held up our treat bags in anticipation. Beside us, the front window glowed. From close up, the jack-o'-lantern's grin appeared to grow wider. We rang the bell again, waited, then rang it again.

"She has to be in there," I said, pointing to the jack-o'-lantern's flickering glow. "She just isn't answering."

"String her," Bill said.

We hadn't tricked anyone all night. The can of liquid string hadn't been touched. Suddenly, my

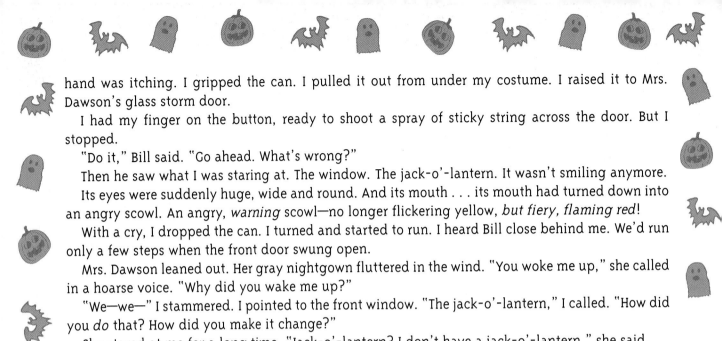

hand was itching. I gripped the can. I pulled it out from under my costume. I raised it to Mrs. Dawson's glass storm door.

I had my finger on the button, ready to shoot a spray of sticky string across the door. But I stopped.

"Do it," Bill said. "Go ahead. What's wrong?"

Then he saw what I was staring at. The window. The jack-o'-lantern. It wasn't smiling anymore.

Its eyes were suddenly huge, wide and round. And its mouth . . . its mouth had turned down into an angry scowl. An angry, *warning* scowl—no longer flickering yellow, *but fiery, flaming red*!

With a cry, I dropped the can. I turned and started to run. I heard Bill close behind me. We'd run only a few steps when the front door swung open.

Mrs. Dawson leaned out. Her gray nightgown fluttered in the wind. "You woke me up," she called in a hoarse voice. "Why did you wake me up?"

"We—we—" I stammered. I pointed to the front window. "The jack-o'-lantern," I called. "How did you *do* that? How did you make it change?"

She stared at me for a long time. "Jack-o'-lantern? I don't have a jack-o'-lantern," she said.

Shivering, I stared at the front window. . . now completely black.

My brother and I talked about that Halloween for years. And each time we retold the story, it got a little scarier. Did it really happen to us? I think so. I really do.

We would have been much safer and happier in the pumpkin patch with Linus. Waiting for the Great Pumpkin would have been all the excitement we needed.

Yes, I'm a scary guy. I like the full-moon thrills and cold shivers of Halloween. But I also like the idea of hoping against hope, dreaming that the impossible can happen. Maybe this year Linus will get his wish. Maybe the Great Pumpkin will finally appear.

For most of my life, I read the *Peanuts* comic strip every day. As a writer, I marveled at Charles Schulz. I pictured him sitting down every morning, facing a blank sheet of paper. I thought of him conjuring up a world so personal to him, but so delightful to millions of people everywhere.

How pleased he must have been when he dreamed up the Great Pumpkin. And how pleased I am to introduce this new Halloween book to you.

Happy Halloween, everyone! And watch out for those grinning jack-o'-lanterns!

—R. L. Stine

"PEANUTS"
BOO!
BOO!
BOO!
Copr. 1951 by United Feature Syndicate Inc
BOO!
THAT SHEET ISN'T VERY WHITE, IS IT, VIOLET ?
MRS. BROWN MUST BE GETTING CARELESS WITH HER WASHING !
BOO!!
RATS !
?
7/2 SCHULZ

7-2-51

"PEANUTS"
BOO!
Copr. 1951 by United Feature Syndicate, Inc.
BOO!
?
7/3 SCHULZ

7-3-51

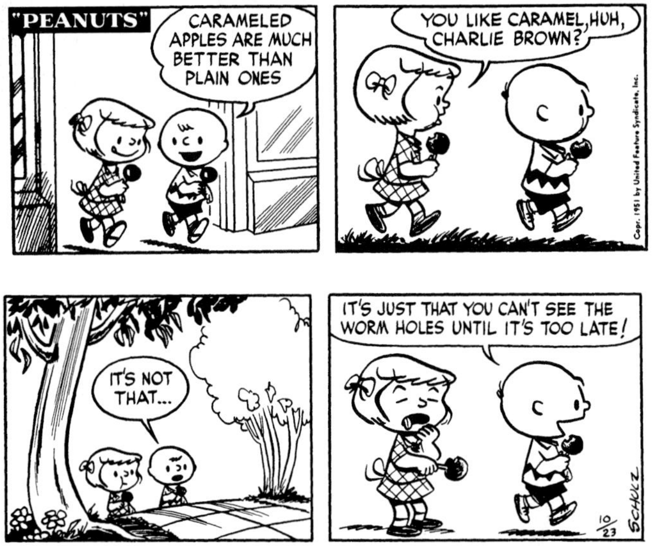
"PEANUTS"
CARAMELED APPLES ARE MUCH BETTER THAN PLAIN ONES
YOU LIKE CARAMEL, HUH, CHARLIE BROWN?
Copr. 1951 by United Feature Syndicate, Inc.
IT'S NOT THAT...
IT'S JUST THAT YOU CAN'T SEE THE WORM HOLES UNTIL IT'S TOO LATE!
10/23
SCHULZ

10-23-51

Caramel Apples

The caramel coating is very gooey, so refrigerate the apples for about 15 minutes, or until the caramel has firmed up. (You will need 6 wooden craft sticks for this recipe.)

- 6 apples
- 1 (14-oz) pkg. individually wrapped caramels, unwrapped
- 2 tablespoons milk

Remove the stem from each apple and press a craft stick into the top. Butter a baking sheet.

Place caramels and milk in a microwave-safe bowl, and microwave 2 minutes, stirring once. Allow to cool briefly.

Roll each apple quickly in caramel sauce until well coated. Place on prepared sheet to set.

Makes 6 caramel apples.

"PEANUTS"
BOO!
BOO!!
?
WE'RE DOING OUR HALLOWEEN GHOSTING EARLY!
ONLY TWO MORE GHOSTING DAYS 'TIL HALLOWEEN!
BOO
Copr. 1951 by United Feature Syndicate, Inc.
10/29
SCHULZ

10-29-51

"PEANUTS"
BOO!
BOO!
Boo!
Boo!
Boo!
Boo!
Boo!
BOO!!
Copr. 1951 by United Feature Syndicate, Inc.
10/31
SCHULZ

10-31-51

"PEANUTS"
KNOCK! KNOCK!
TRICKS OR TREATS... MONEY OR EATS!
WHAT?!
Copr. 1951 by United Feature Syndicate, Inc.
GET OUT OF HERE!!! HALLOWEEN WAS YESTERDAY!
I'M STILL HUNGRY!
SLAM!
11/1
SCHULZ

11-1-51

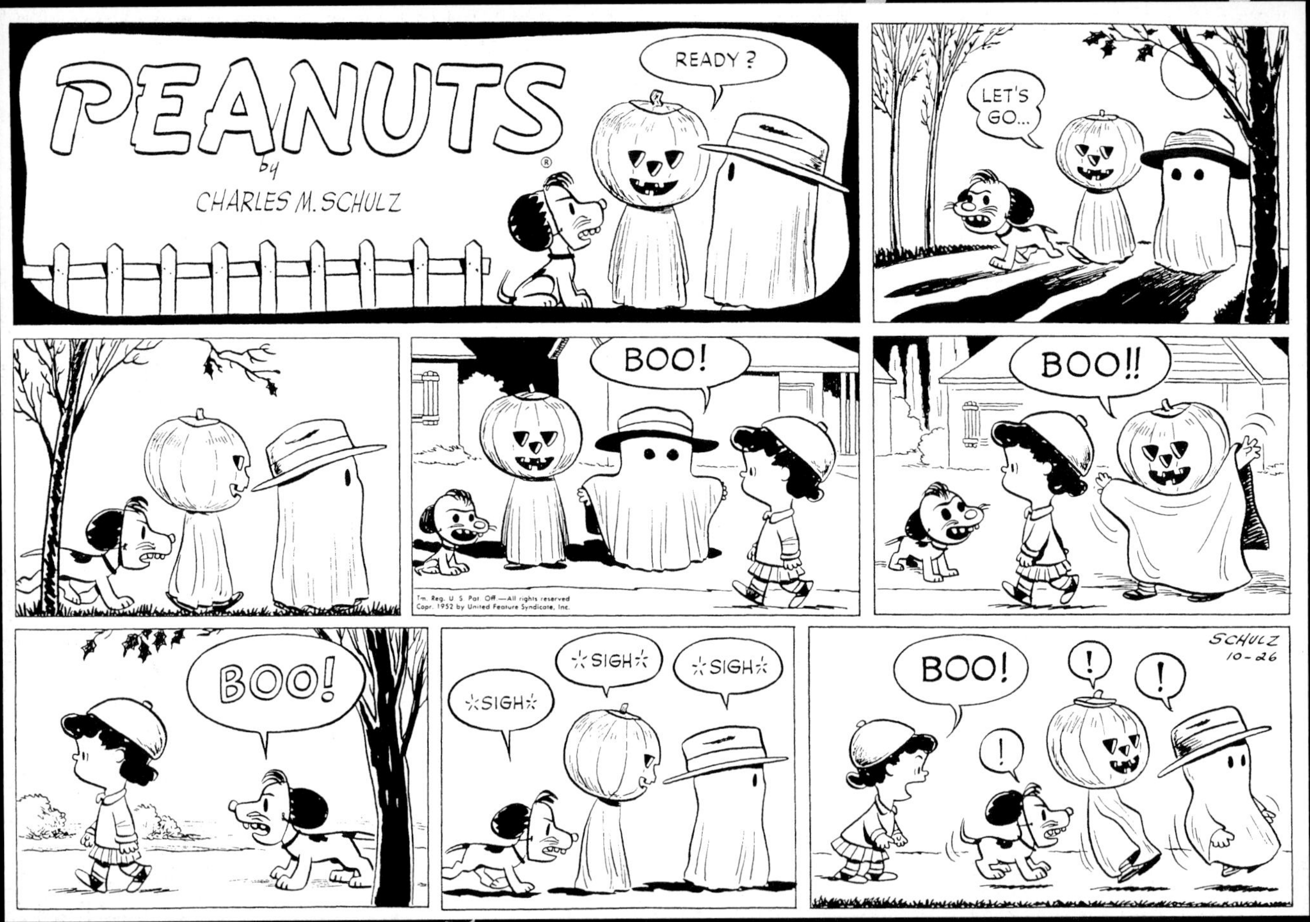
PEANUTS
by
CHARLES M. SCHULZ
READY ?
LET'S GO...
BOO!
BOO!!
Tm. Reg. U. S. Pat. Off.—All rights reserved
Copr. 1952 by United Feature Syndicate, Inc.
BOO!
SIGH
SIGH
SIGH
BOO!
!
!
!
SCHULZ
10-26

10-26-52

"PEANUTS"
"TRICKS OR TREATS, MONEY OR EATS!"
GO AHEAD! DO YOUR WORST! WE DON'T CARE!
SIGH
Tm. Reg. U. S. Pat. Off.—All rights reserved Copr. 1952 by United Feature Syndicate, Inc.
SCHULZ
10-31

10-31-52

"PEANUTS"
BOO!
OH, TAKE THAT SHEET OFF, CHARLIE BROWN...
BOO!
HALLOWEEN WAS YESTERDAY
BOO
Tm. Reg. U. S. Pat. Off.—All rights reserved Copr. 1952 by United Feature Syndicate, Inc.
OUR LAUNDRY DIDN'T COME BACK UNTIL TODAY
11-1
SCHULZ

11-1-52

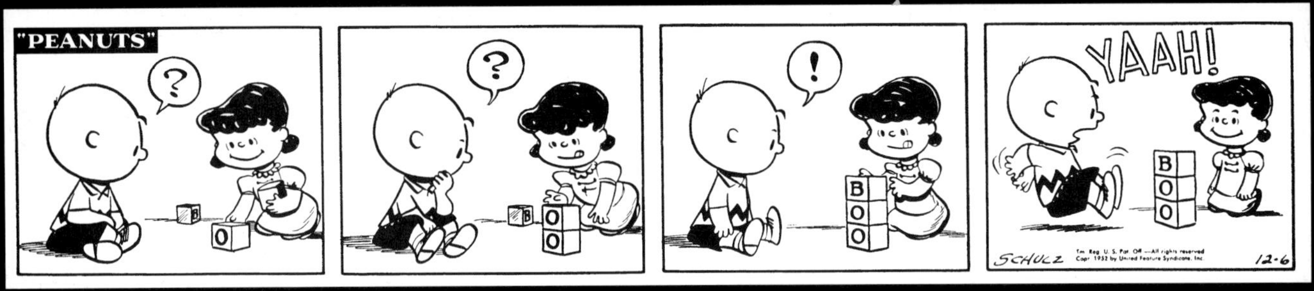
"PEANUTS"
?
O
?
O
O
!
B
O
O
YAAH!
B
O
O
SCHULZ
Tm Reg. U. S. Pat. Off.—All rights reserved
Copr. 1952 by United Feature Syndicate, Inc.
12-6

12-6-52

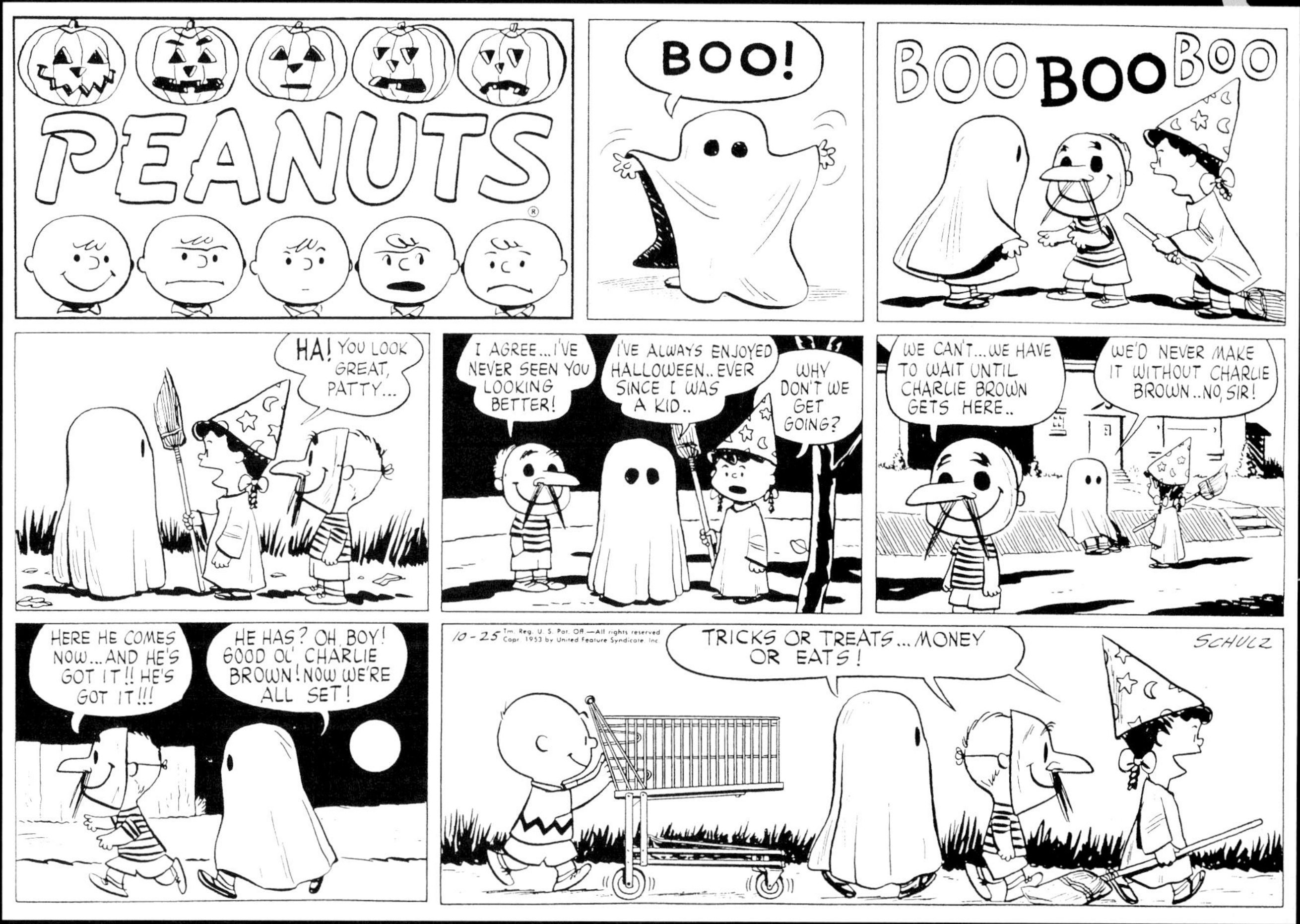
PEANUTS
BOO!
BOO BOO BOO
HA! YOU LOOK GREAT, PATTY...
I AGREE...I'VE NEVER SEEN YOU LOOKING BETTER!
I'VE ALWAYS ENJOYED HALLOWEEN..EVER SINCE I WAS A KID..
WHY DON'T WE GET GOING?
WE CAN'T...WE HAVE TO WAIT UNTIL CHARLIE BROWN GETS HERE..
WE'D NEVER MAKE IT WITHOUT CHARLIE BROWN..NO, SIR!
HERE HE COMES NOW...AND HE'S GOT IT!! HE'S GOT IT!!!
HE HAS? OH, BOY! GOOD OL' CHARLIE BROWN! NOW WE'RE ALL SET!
10-25 Tm. Reg. U. S. Pat. Off.—All rights reserved Copr. 1953 by United Feature Syndicate, Inc.
SCHULZ
TRICKS OR TREATS...MONEY OR EATS!

10-25-53

Charlie Brown's Halloween Ghost Costume

- 1 white twin-size sheet if you're a kid

OR

- 1 white full-size sheet if you're an adult

- 1 pair of scissors

A weird and wacky take on the traditional ghost costume, the "Charlie Brown Ghost" is a wonderful costume for trick-or-treating. Hopefully you will get better treats than rocks!

Take your sheet and scissors and cut several holes throughout the sheet. To cut holes, fold over sheet and at the crease cut a C shape. Make sure you cut 2 holes for your eyes.

PEANUTS
IS THAT YOU, LUCY?
UH, HUH... LINUS WILL BE ALONG IN A MINUTE...
HE WAS HAVING A LITTLE TROUBLE WITH HIS COSTUME..
?
HE'S NOT VERY GOOD YET WITH A SCISSORS!
10-31
SCHULZ

10-31-56

"PEANUTS"
BOO!
BOO!
SCHULZ 10-28
Tm. Reg. U. S. Pat. Off.—All rights reserved Copr. 1953 by United Feature Syndicate, Inc.

10-28-53

"PEANUTS"
I'LL GO UP TO EACH HOUSE, SEE? AND I'LL SHOUT 'TRICKS OR TREATS!'
WHAT WILL YOU DO IF THEY DON'T GIVE YOU ANYTHING?
OH, I'LL MAKE 'EM WISH THEY HAD! YES, SIR!
BOY, WHAT I WON'T DO TO 'EM! YES, SIR! I'LL... I'LL JUST... I'LL.. I'LL... I'LL.... I'LL....
I'LL RING THEIR DOORBELL!
10/29
SCHULZ
Tm. Reg. U. S. Pat. Off.—All rights reserved Copr. 1953 by United Feature Syndicate, Inc.

10-29-53

"PEANUTS"
BOO!
BOO!
KLUNK!
RATS
I GIVE UP!
YOU JUST CAN'T BE A GHOST IN A CONTOUR SHEET!
10-31
SCHULZ

10-31-53

"PEANUTS"
CHOMP-CHOMP GULP
WELL, THAT'S THE LAST OF IT...
?
THAT'S THE LAST OF WHAT ?
MY HALLOWEEN CANDY!
12/2
SCHULZ

12-2-53

"PEANUTS"

THERE'S ONLY ONE THING MORE USELESS THAN YESTERDAY'S NEWSPAPER..

WHAT'S THAT?

11-1

YESTERDAY'S HALLOWEEN PUMPKIN!

SCHULZ

11-1-54

"PEANUTS"
DO YOU THINK IT WOULD BE ALL RIGHT TO WEAR THIS ON HALLOWEEN, CHARLIE BROWN?
SURE, WHY NOT?
I JUST THOUGHT MAYBE SOME **REAL** GHOST MIGHT RESENT IT..
OH, DON'T WORRY ABOUT THAT LUCY... DON'T WORRY ABOUT THAT...
WELL, I DON'T WANNA GET **SUED**, YOU KNOW!
SCHULZ
10-28

10-28-55

"PEANUTS"
BOO!
OH, GOOD GRIEF!
YOU CAN'T SCARE ANYONE IN BROAD DAYLIGHT, LUCY!
WHAT DO YOU MEAN, BROAD DAYLIGHT?
IT'S DARK IN **HERE**!
10-29
SCHULZ

10-29-55

Trick-or-Treat Bag

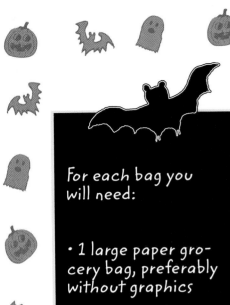

For each bag you will need:

- 1 large paper grocery bag, preferably without graphics
- ¼-inch-hole paper punch
- clear nail polish (optional)
- rubber stamps and inks
- stickers
- glitter pen (optional)
- 18-inch-long twine, leather, or ribbon

A run-of-the-mill paper grocery bag is transformed into a fanciful Halloween treat bag with the help of rubber stamps, stickers, and, if you please, a glitter pen. Let your imagination run wild when you decorate—the scarier, the merrier! Children will need help folding and hole punching the bag.

Fold down the top of the bag three times, making a sturdy 2-inch-wide band. Punch 2 holes, one at each end, into the band. Adults can reinforce the bag by using the clear nail polish to paint a 1/4-inch-wide border around the holes, both inside and outside the bag.

Using rubber stamps, stickers, or a glitter pen, decorate the bag. Let the ink dry. Thread the twine, leather, or ribbon through the holes in the band, then tie to secure, forming a secure handle.

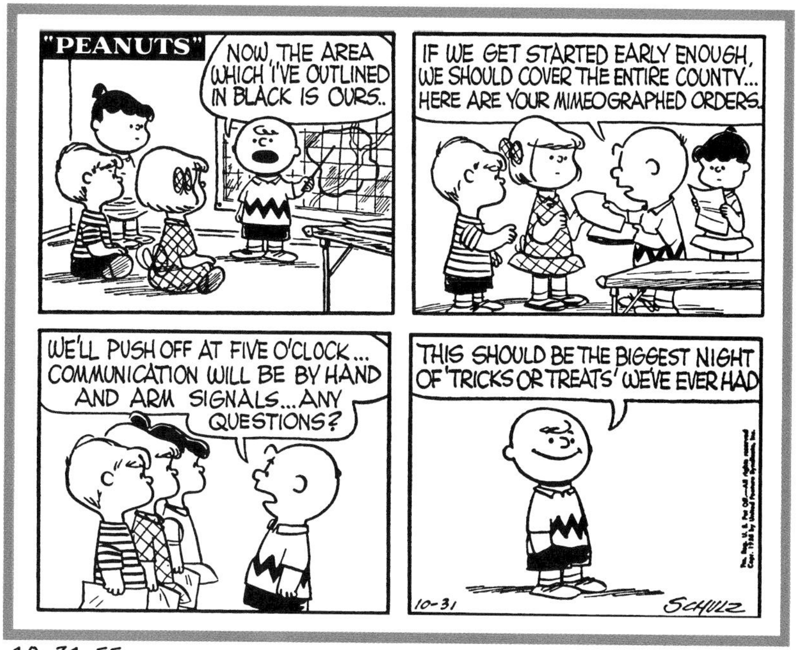
"PEANUTS"
NOW, THE AREA WHICH I'VE OUTLINED IN BLACK IS OURS..
IF WE GET STARTED EARLY ENOUGH, WE SHOULD COVER THE ENTIRE COUNTY... HERE ARE YOUR MIMEOGRAPHED ORDERS.
WE'LL PUSH OFF AT FIVE O'CLOCK... COMMUNICATION WILL BE BY HAND AND ARM SIGNALS...ANY QUESTIONS?
THIS SHOULD BE THE BIGGEST NIGHT OF 'TRICKS OR TREATS' WE'VE EVER HAD
10-31
SCHULZ

10-31-55

"PEANUTS"
RING
TRICKS OR TREATS!
WHAT?!
I'VE BEEN AWAY..
11-14
SCHULZ

11-14-55

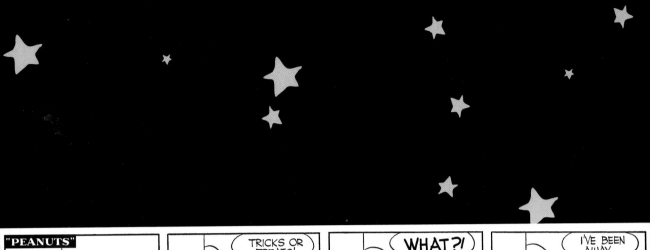

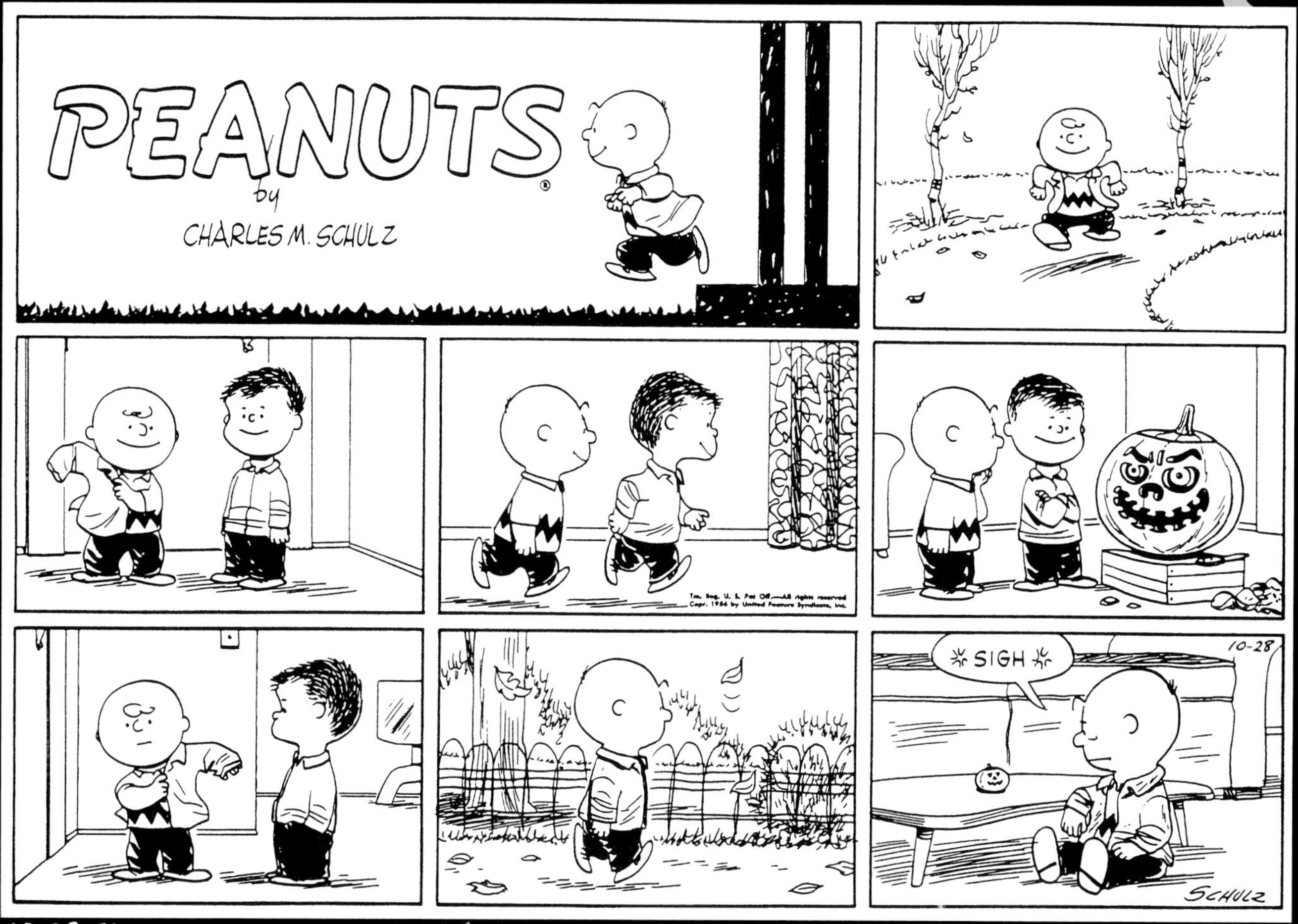
PEANUTS
by
CHARLES M. SCHULZ
Tm. Reg. U. S. Pat Off.—All rights reserved
Copr. 1956 by United Feature Syndicate, Inc.
SIGH
10-28
SCHULZ

10-28-56

PEANUTS
I WAS JUST THINKING ABOUT HALLOWEEN, CHARLIE BROWN...
AND THEN I GOT TO THINKING ABOUT PUMPKINS, AND THEN, OF COURSE, I WAS REMINDED OF YOUR ROUND HEAD
AND THEN I GOT TO THINKING WHAT A SHAME IT IS THAT YOUR HEAD ISN'T SORT OF AN ORANGE COLOR BECAUSE...
ALL RIGHT!!!
10-29
SCHULZ

10-29-56

PEANUTS
NOW, YOU KNOW WHAT YOU'RE GOING TO DO TOMORROW NIGHT, DON'T YOU?
SURE..I JUST GO UP TO THESE DIFFERENT HOUSES, RING THEIR DOORBELLS AND THEN SHOUT, "TRICKS OR TREATS!"
SAY, BY THE WAY... THERE'S NO LAW AGAINST THAT, IS THERE?
OF COURSE NOT..
I WOULDN'T WANT TO DO ANYTHING THAT MIGHT AROUSE THE F.B.I.!
10-30
SCHULZ

10-30-56

PEANUTS
BOY, WHAT A DOPE HE TURNED OUT TO BE!
I TAKE HIM OUT FOR "TRICKS OR TREATS," AND HE GETS **STAGE FRIGHT**! HE JUST **STOOD** THERE!! HE WOULDN'T SAY A **WORD**!!!
SIGH
JUST WAIT 'TIL NEXT YEAR!!
11-1
SCHULZ

11-1-56

PEANUTS
LOOK! HERE'S SCHROEDER'S OLD HALLOWEEN PUMPKIN!
HOW DO YOU KNOW THAT WAS HIS? HALLOWEEN WAS FIVE WEEKS AGO! HOW CAN YOU REMEMBER?
OH, I REMEMBER, ALL RIGHT...
Tm. Reg. U. S. Pat. Off.—All rights reserved Copr. 1956 by United Feature Syndicate, Inc.
I'M NOT SO GOOD AT NAMES, BUT I NEVER FORGET A FACE!
12-3
SCHULZ

12-3-56

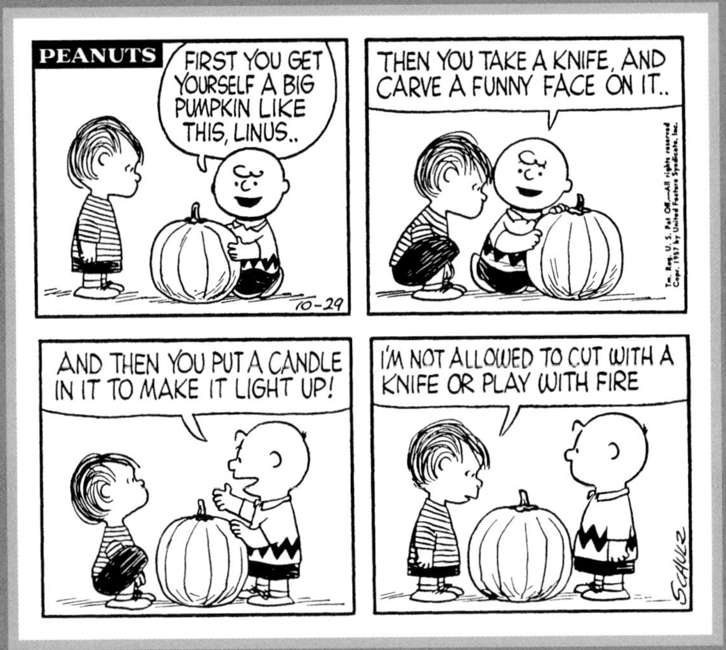
PEANUTS
FIRST YOU GET YOURSELF A BIG PUMPKIN LIKE THIS, LINUS..
10-29
THEN YOU TAKE A KNIFE, AND CARVE A FUNNY FACE ON IT..
AND THEN YOU PUT A CANDLE IN IT TO MAKE IT LIGHT UP!
I'M NOT ALLOWED TO CUT WITH A KNIFE OR PLAY WITH FIRE
SCHULZ

10-29-57

Paper Bag Pumpkin

Here's a fat and jolly pumpkin to sit on your mantle or table. Kids will have fun crumpling the newpaper and stuffing the bag. Younger pixies can use their hands to paint the pumpkin; older children can use the paint brushes.

Fill the lunch bag with the crumpled newspaper, filling out the sides so it forms a pumpkin shape. Gather together the top of the bag to form a 1-inch stem. Secure with a rubber band.

Paint the entire bag, except the stem, with the orange paint. Paint the stem green. Use the black paint to paint the features of the jack-o'-lantern.

For each pumpkin you will need:

- paper lunch bag, preferably white
- newspaper, crumpled
- rubber band
- orange, black, and green tempera paints
- paint brushes

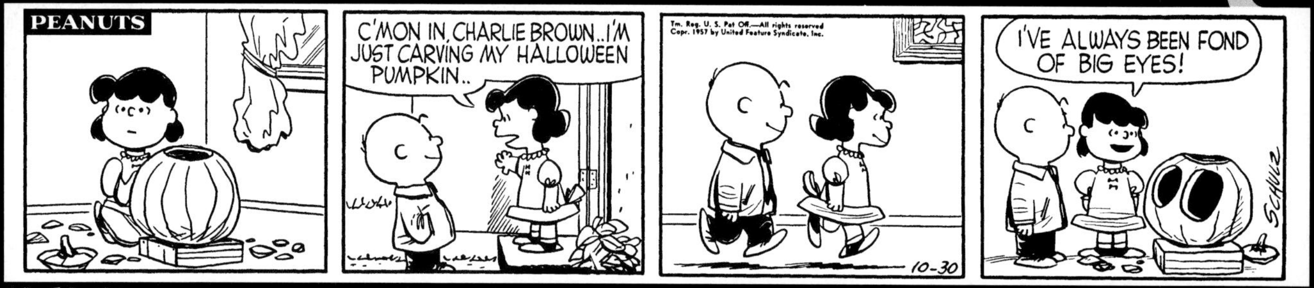
PEANUTS
C'MON IN, CHARLIE BROWN.. I'M JUST CARVING MY HALLOWEEN PUMPKIN..
Tm. Reg. U. S. Pat. Off.—All rights reserved Copr. 1957 by United Feature Syndicate, Inc.
10-30
I'VE ALWAYS BEEN FOND OF BIG EYES!
SCHULZ

10-30-57

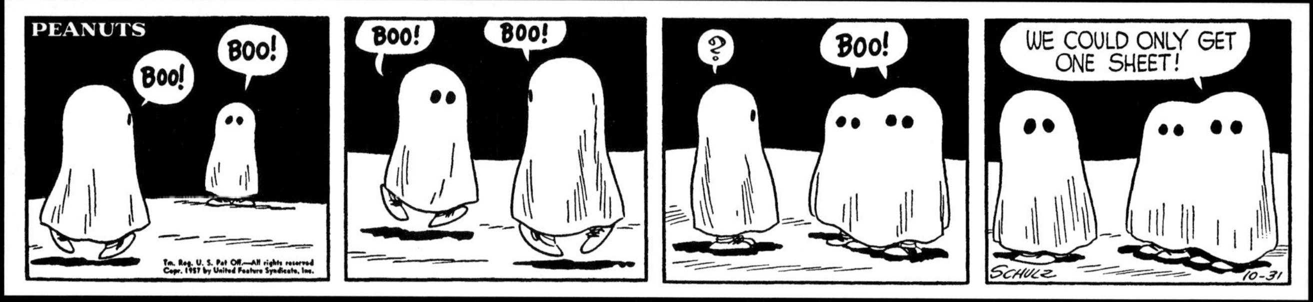
PEANUTS
BOO!
BOO!
Tm. Reg. U. S. Pat. Off.—All rights reserved Copr. 1957 by United Feature Syndicate, Inc.
BOO!
BOO!
?
BOO!
WE COULD ONLY GET ONE SHEET!
SCHULZ
10-31

10-30-57

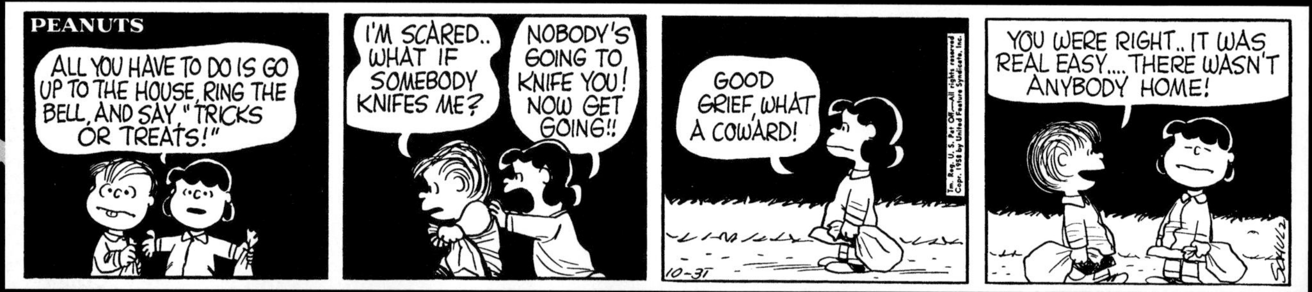
PEANUTS
ALL YOU HAVE TO DO IS GO UP TO THE HOUSE, RING THE BELL, AND SAY "TRICKS OR TREATS!"
I'M SCARED.. WHAT IF SOMEBODY KNIFES ME?
NOBODY'S GOING TO KNIFE YOU! NOW GET GOING!!
GOOD GRIEF, WHAT A COWARD!
Tm. Reg. U. S. Pat. Off.—All rights reserved Copr. 1958 by United Feature Syndicate, Inc.
10-31
YOU WERE RIGHT.. IT WAS REAL EASY.... THERE WASN'T ANYBODY HOME!
SCHULZ

10-31-58

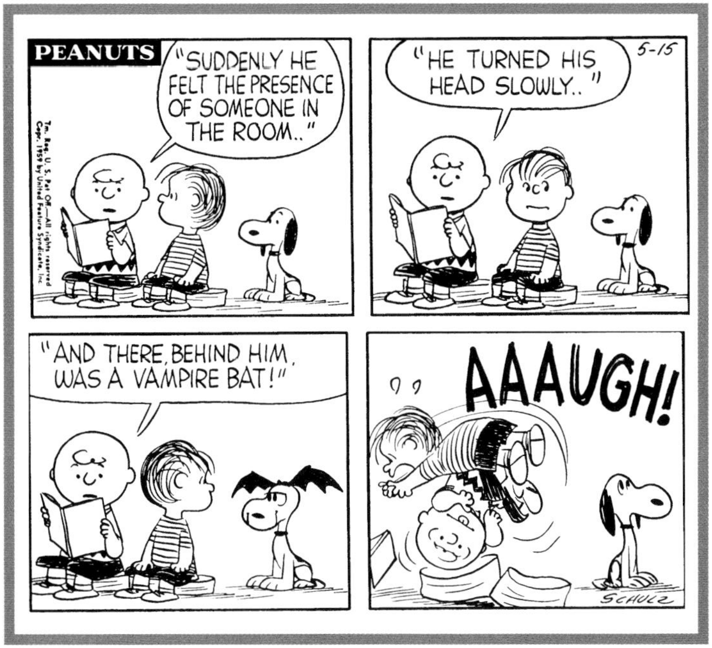
PEANUTS
"SUDDENLY HE FELT THE PRESENCE OF SOMEONE IN THE ROOM.."
5-15
"HE TURNED HIS HEAD SLOWLY.."
"AND THERE, BEHIND HIM, WAS A VAMPIRE BAT!"
AAAUGH!
SCHULZ

5-15-59

Fanciful Masks

For each mask you will need:

- 1 plain dime-store mask (white or black)
- clear-drying craft glue

Dime-store masks take on fanciful personalities (as do people who wear them) when decorated with seasonal items and natural finds. Kids can create simple collage masks while older children (including adults) can create more sophisticated masks.

Possible decorations:
Small autumn leaves (collect them at least 1 week prior to making the mask); wax or paper wrappers from bite-size candies such as Tootsie Rolls™ and Mary Janes™, twisted in the center to form a bow; stickers; Indian corn or colored popcorn (unpopped); sequins; feathers; fabric trim such as pom-poms.

Have the mask ready, along with the objects that you are using to decorate the mask. Working with one decoration at a time, spread glue onto the back and arrange on the mask. Begin at the outer edge of the mask and work inward, covering the surface completely. When you get to the eye holes, either fold the edges of the flat objects toward the back of the mask or trim them. Let the mask dry completely before wearing.

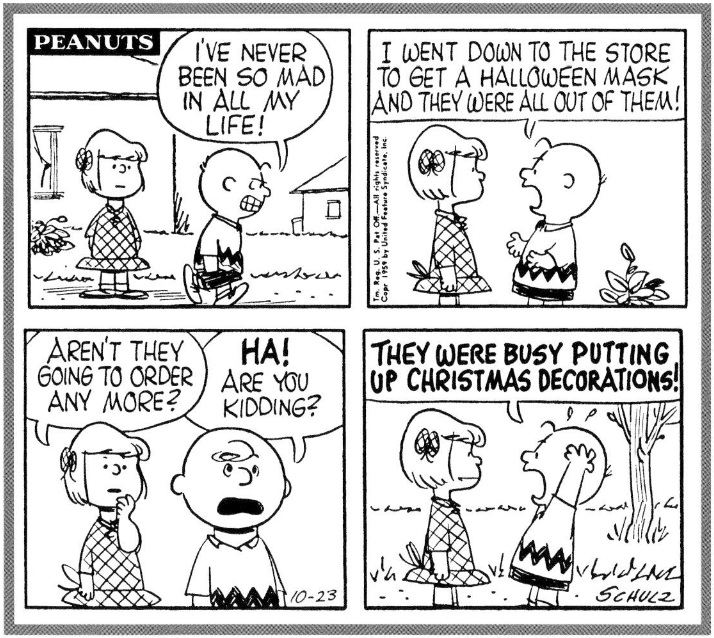
PEANUTS
I'VE NEVER BEEN SO MAD IN ALL MY LIFE!
I WENT DOWN TO THE STORE TO GET A HALLOWEEN MASK AND THEY WERE ALL OUT OF THEM!
Tm. Reg. U. S. Pat. Off.—All rights reserved
Copr. 1959 by United Feature Syndicate, Inc.
AREN'T THEY GOING TO ORDER ANY MORE?
HA! ARE YOU KIDDING?
10-23
THEY WERE BUSY PUTTING UP CHRISTMAS DECORATIONS!
SCHULZ

10-23-59

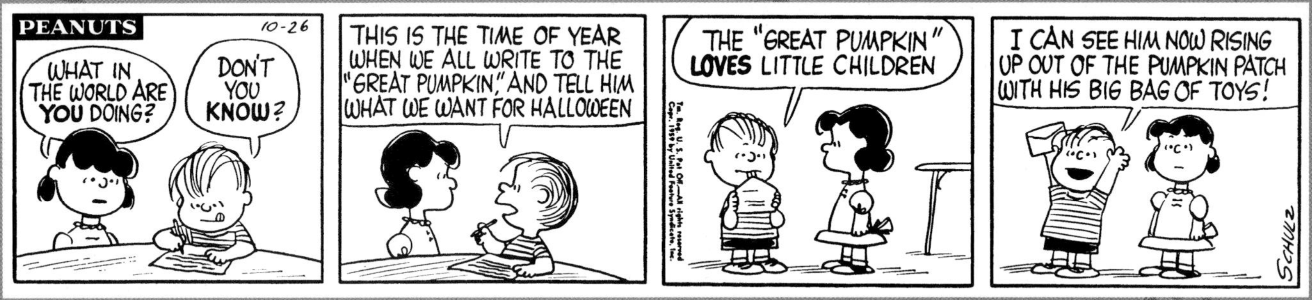
PEANUTS
10-26
WHAT IN THE WORLD ARE **YOU** DOING?
DON'T YOU **KNOW**?
THIS IS THE TIME OF YEAR WHEN WE ALL WRITE TO THE "GREAT PUMPKIN," AND TELL HIM WHAT WE WANT FOR HALLOWEEN
THE "GREAT PUMPKIN" **LOVES** LITTLE CHILDREN
I CAN SEE HIM NOW RISING UP OUT OF THE PUMPKIN PATCH WITH HIS BIG BAG OF TOYS!
SCHULZ

10-26-59

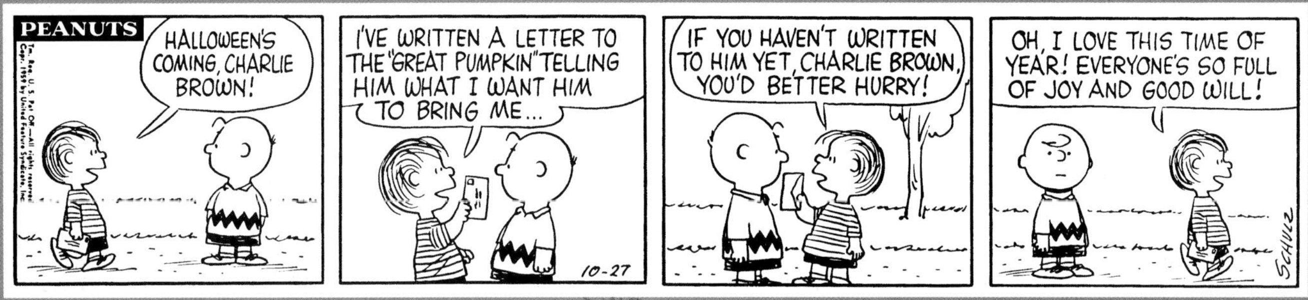
PEANUTS
HALLOWEEN'S COMING, CHARLIE BROWN!
I'VE WRITTEN A LETTER TO THE "GREAT PUMPKIN" TELLING HIM WHAT I WANT HIM TO BRING ME...
10-27
IF YOU HAVEN'T WRITTEN TO HIM YET, CHARLIE BROWN, YOU'D BETTER HURRY!
OH, I LOVE THIS TIME OF YEAR! EVERYONE'S SO FULL OF JOY AND GOOD WILL!
SCHULZ

10-27-59

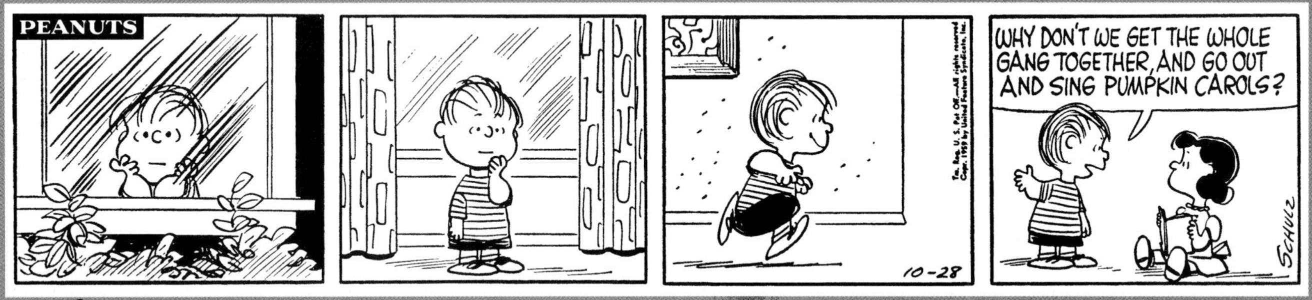
PEANUTS
10-28
WHY DON'T WE GET THE WHOLE GANG TOGETHER, AND GO OUT AND SING PUMPKIN CAROLS?
SCHULZ

10-28-59

PEANUTS
...AND THEN ON HALLOWEEN NIGHT THE "GREAT PUMPKIN" RISES UP OUT OF THE PUMPKIN PATCH...
..AND HE BRINGS TOYS TO ALL THE GOOD LITTLE CHILDREN IN THE WORLD!
YOU'RE CRAZY!
ALL RIGHT, SO YOU BELIEVE IN SANTA CLAUS, AND I'LL BELIEVE IN THE "GREAT PUMPKIN"..
THE WAY I SEE IT, IT DOESN'T MATTER WHAT YOU BELIEVE JUST SO YOU'RE SINCERE!
10-29
SCHULZ

10-29-59

PEANUTS
TOMORROW NIGHT IS OUR BIG NIGHT, LINUS..
ALL YOU HAVE TO DO IS WALK UP TO A HOUSE, RING THE DOORBELL AND SAY, "TRICKS OR TREATS!"
ARE YOU SURE THAT'S LEGAL?
OF COURSE, IT'S LEGAL!
GOOD...I WOULDN'T WANT TO BE ACCUSED OF TAKING PART IN A RUMBLE!
10-30
SCHULZ

10-30-59

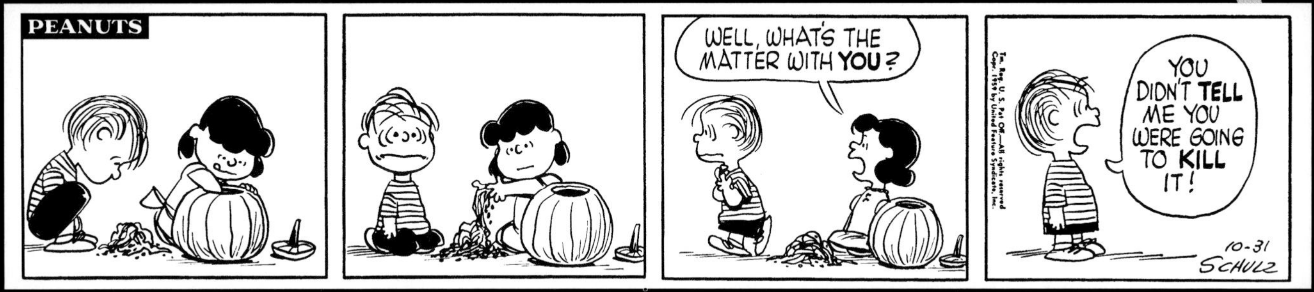
PEANUTS
WELL, WHAT'S THE MATTER WITH YOU?
YOU DIDN'T TELL ME YOU WERE GOING TO KILL IT!
Tm. Reg. U. S. Pat. Off.—All rights reserved Copr. 1959 by United Feature Syndicate, Inc.
10-31
SCHULZ

10-31-59

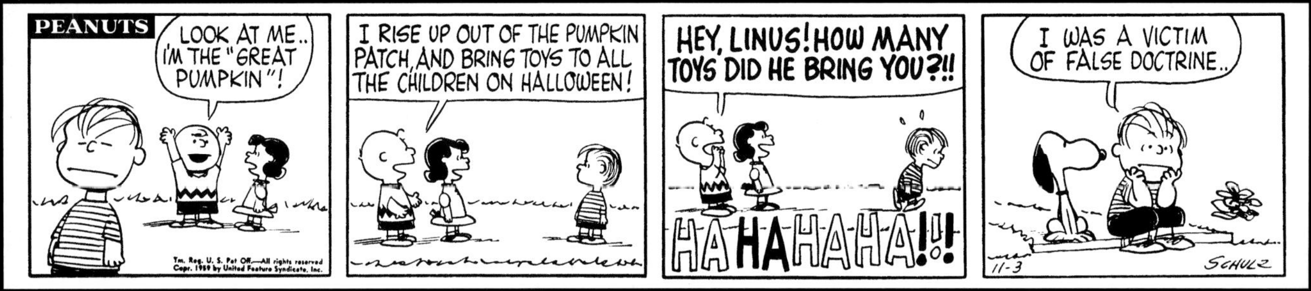
PEANUTS
LOOK AT ME.. I'M THE "GREAT PUMPKIN"!
Tm. Reg. U. S. Pat. Off.—All rights reserved Copr. 1959 by United Feature Syndicate, Inc.
I RISE UP OUT OF THE PUMPKIN PATCH, AND BRING TOYS TO ALL THE CHILDREN ON HALLOWEEN!
HEY, LINUS! HOW MANY TOYS DID HE BRING YOU?!!
HAHAHAHAHA!!!
I WAS A VICTIM OF FALSE DOCTRINE..
11-3
SCHULZ

11-3-59

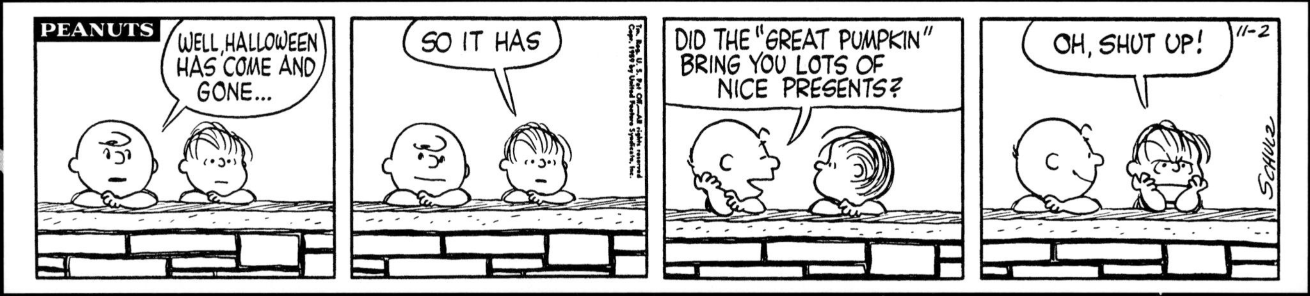
PEANUTS
WELL, HALLOWEEN HAS COME AND GONE...
SO IT HAS
Tm. Reg. U. S. Pat. Off.—All rights reserved Copr. 1959 by United Feature Syndicate, Inc.
DID THE "GREAT PUMPKIN" BRING YOU LOTS OF NICE PRESENTS?
OH, SHUT UP!
11-2
SCHULZ

11-2-59

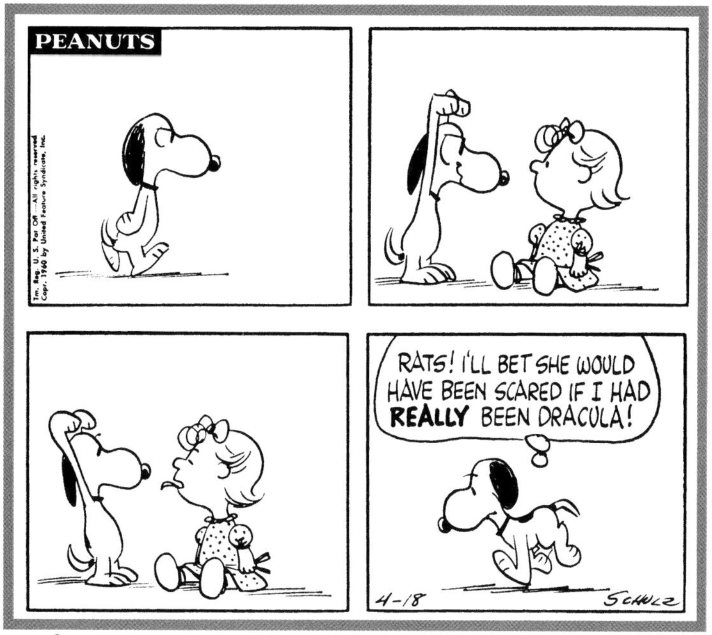
PEANUTS
Tm. Reg. U. S. Pat. Off.—All rights reserved
Copr. 1960 by United Feature Syndicate, Inc.
RATS! I'LL BET SHE WOULD HAVE BEEN SCARED IF I HAD **REALLY** BEEN DRACULA!
4-18
SCHULZ

4-18-60

PEANUTS
Tm. Reg. U. S. Pat Off.—All rights reserved Copr. 1961 by United Feature Syndicate, Inc.
HERE'S A GHOST STORY I THINK YOU'LL LIKE, LINUS...
IT'S REAL INTERESTING, BUT YET IT ISN'T TOO SCARY...
YOU WERE RIGHT...IT WAS ONLY MILDLY FRIGHTENING!
6-30
SCHULZ

6-30-61

PEANUTS
HERE COMES THE LITTLE BABY WITH HIS BLANKET
HEE! HEE! HEE! LOOK AT THE LITTLE BABY...HE HAS TO HAVE A BLANKET!
Tm. Reg. U. S. Pat Off.—All rights reserved Copr. 1961 by United Feature Syndicate, Inc.
I AM THE COUNT DRACULA FROM TRANSYLVANIA
7-18
AAUGH!
SCHULZ

7-18-61

PEANUTS
..AND THEN, SALLY, ON HALLOWEEN NIGHT, THE GREAT PUMPKIN APPEARS!
HE FLIES THROUGH THE AIR, AND BRINGS TOYS TO ALL THE CHILDREN OF THE WORLD!
HA!
10-24
I DON'T THINK SHE BELIEVED ME...
Tm. Reg. U. S. Pat. Off.—All rights reserved
Copr. 1961 by United Feature Syndicate, Inc.
SCHULZ

10-24-61

PEANUTS
Tm. Reg. U. S. Pat. Off.—All rights reserved
Copr. 1961 by United Feature Syndicate, Inc.
YOU'RE CRAZY! YOU'RE JUST PLAIN STUPID CRAZY!
YOU TALK LIKE SOMEONE WHO'S JUST FALLEN OUT OF A TREE! YOU'RE STARK RAVING STUPID!!
10-25
I SHOULD HAVE KNOWN BETTER...
THERE ARE THREE THINGS I HAVE LEARNED NEVER TO DISCUSS WITH PEOPLE...RELIGION, POLITICS AND THE GREAT PUMPKIN!
SCHULZ

10-25-61

PEANUTS
ISN'T LINUS GOING OUT FOR "TRICKS OR TREATS"?
NO, HE'S SITTING IN THE PUMPKIN PATCH WAITING FOR THE GREAT PUMPKIN TO APPEAR
10-31
WELL, WHEN YOU GO UP TO THIS NEXT HOUSE, ASK THE LADY FOR AN EXTRA TREAT FOR YOUR LITTLE BROTHER WHO IS SITTING OUT IN THE PUMPKIN PATCH
Reg. U. S. Pat. Off.—All rights reserved Copr. 1961 by United Feature Syndicate, Inc.
ALL I GOT FROM HER WAS A VERY PECULIAR LOOK!
SCHULZ

10-31-61

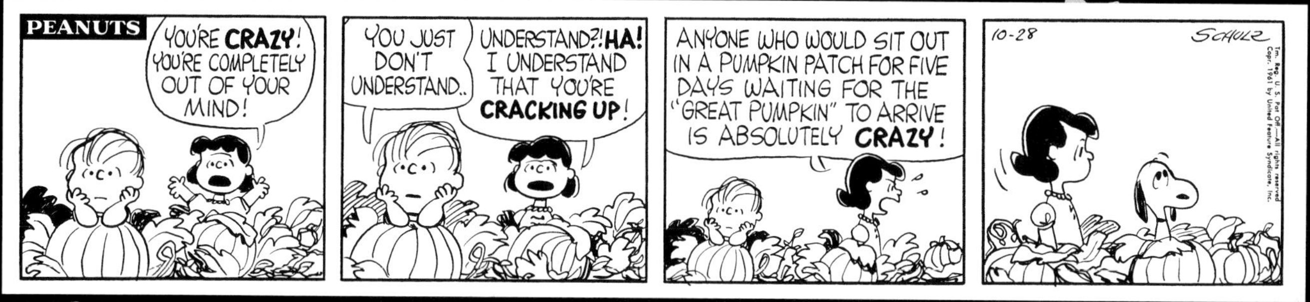
PEANUTS
YOU'RE **CRAZY**! YOU'RE COMPLETELY OUT OF YOUR MIND!
YOU JUST DON'T UNDERSTAND..
UNDERSTAND?! **HA!** I UNDERSTAND THAT YOU'RE **CRACKING UP**!
ANYONE WHO WOULD SIT OUT IN A PUMPKIN PATCH FOR FIVE DAYS WAITING FOR THE "GREAT PUMPKIN" TO ARRIVE IS ABSOLUTELY **CRAZY**!
10-28
SCHULZ
Tm. Reg. U. S. Pat Off.—All rights reserved
Copr. 1961 by United Feature Syndicate, Inc.

10-28-61

Black Bottom Cups

- 2 (3-oz) pkg. cream cheese, softened
- $1/3$ cup sugar
- 1 egg
- 1 (6-oz) pkg. (1 cup) semisweet chocolate chips
- 1 $1/2$ cups all purpose flour
- 1 cup sugar
- $1/4$ cup unsweetened cocoa
- 1 teaspoon baking soda
- $1/2$ teaspoon salt
- 1 cup water
- $1/3$ cup oil
- 1 tablespoon vinegar
- 1 teaspoon vanilla
- $1/2$ cup chopped almonds, if desired
- 2 tablespoons sugar, if desired

Everyone loves cupcakes on Halloween! Whether it's for your local bake sale, party attendees, or your favorite trick-or-treaters, this recipe is sure to please.

Heat oven to 350°F. Line 18 muffin cups with paper baking cups. In a small bowl, combine cream cheese, 1/3 cup sugar, and egg; blend well. Stir in chocolate chips. Set aside.

In a large bowl, combine flour, 1 cup sugar, cocoa, baking soda, and salt; mix well. Add water, oil, vinegar, and vanilla; beat 2 minutes at medium speed.

Fill paper-lined muffin cups half full. Top each with 1 tablespoon cream cheese mixture. Combine almonds and 2 tablespoons sugar; sprinkle evenly over cream cheese mixture.

Bake at 350°F for 20 to 30 minutes or until cream cheese mixture is light golden brown. Cool 15 minutes. Remove from pans. Let sit for 30 minutes or until completely cooled. Store in refrigerator.

Decoration Note—In addition to or in place of the almond-sugar mixture topping, you can top each cupcake with your favorite Halloween candy or sprinkles.

Makes 18 cupcakes.

PEANUTS

DEAR GREAT PUMPKIN, I AM LOOKING FORWARD TO YOUR ARRIVAL ON HALLOWEEN NIGHT.

I HOPE YOU WILL BRING ME LOTS OF PRESENTS.

10-13

EVERYONE TELLS ME YOU ARE A FAKE, BUT I BELIEVE IN YOU.

SINCERELY, LINUS VAN PELT

P.S. IF YOU REALLY ARE A FAKE, DON'T TELL ME. I DON'T WANT TO KNOW.

SCHULZ

10-13-62

PEANUTS

AND ON HALLOWEEN NIGHT THE "GREAT PUMPKIN" RISES OUT OF THE PUMPKIN PATCH...

THEN HE FLIES THROUGH THE AIR TO BRING TOYS TO ALL THE GOOD LITTLE CHILDREN EVERYWHERE!

THAT'S A GOOD STORY...

I PLACE IT JUST A LITTLE BELOW THE ONE ABOUT THE FLYING REINDEER!

10-29-62

PEANUTS

ALL RIGHT, SALLY...YOU WANT PROOF...YOU'RE GOING TO GET IT...

WE'LL JUST SIT HERE IN THIS PUMPKIN PATCH, AND YOU'LL SEE THE "GREAT PUMPKIN" WITH YOUR OWN EYES!

IF YOU TRY TO HOLD MY HAND, I'LL SLUG YOU!!

10-31-62

44

PEANUTS
Tm. Reg. U. S. Pat. Off.—All rights reserved Copr. 1962 by United Feature Syndicate, Inc.
HALLOWEEN IS OVER!! I'VE MISSED IT!!!
YOU BLOCKHEAD, YOU'VE KEPT ME UP ALL NIGHT WAITING FOR THE "GREAT PUMPKIN," AND HE NEVER CAME!
I DIDN'T GET A CHANCE TO GO OUT FOR "TRICKS OR TREATS"! IT WAS ALL YOUR FAULT!
I'LL SUE!!
SCHULZ
11-1

11-1-62

PEANUTS
I WAS ROBBED!
I SPENT THE WHOLE NIGHT WAITING FOR THE "GREAT PUMPKIN" WHEN I COULD HAVE BEEN OUT FOR "TRICKS OR TREATS"
YOU'VE HEARD ABOUT FURY AND A WOMAN SCORNED, HAVEN'T YOU?
YES, I GUESS I HAVE...
Tm. Reg. U. S. Pat. Off.—All rights reserved Copr. 1962 by United Feature Syndicate, Inc.
11-2
WELL, THAT'S NOTHING COMPARED TO THE FURY OF A WOMAN WHO HAS BEEN CHEATED OUT OF "TRICKS OR TREATS"!
SCHULZ

11-2-62

PEANUTS
DON'T TELL ME YOU'RE SITTING HERE WAITING FOR THE "GREAT PUMPKIN" AGAIN?
HOW CAN YOU BELIEVE IN SOMETHING THAT JUST ISN'T TRUE? HE'S NEVER GOING TO SHOW UP! HE DOESN'T EXIST!
WHEN YOU STOP BELIEVING IN THAT FELLOW WITH THE RED SUIT AND WHITE BEARD WHO GOES, "HO HO HO," I'LL STOP BELIEVING IN THE "GREAT PUMPKIN"!
10-28
WE ARE OBVIOUSLY SEPARATED BY DENOMINATIONAL DIFFERENCES!
SCHULZ

10-28-63

PEANUTS
STILL WAITING FOR THE "GREAT PUMPKIN"?
UH HUH..WHERE HAVE YOU BEEN, OUT FOR TRICKS OR TREATS?
YEAH, I GOT A WHOLE BAG OF JUNK..DO YOU WANT AN APPLE?
THANK YOU.. IF THE "GREAT PUMPKIN" COMES, I'LL PUT IN A GOOD WORD FOR YOU...
"IF"?
I MEANT, "WHEN"
I'M DOOMED! ONE LITTLE SLIP LIKE THAT CAN CAUSE THE "GREAT PUMPKIN" TO PASS YOU BY!
10-31
SCHULZ

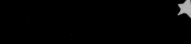

10-31-63

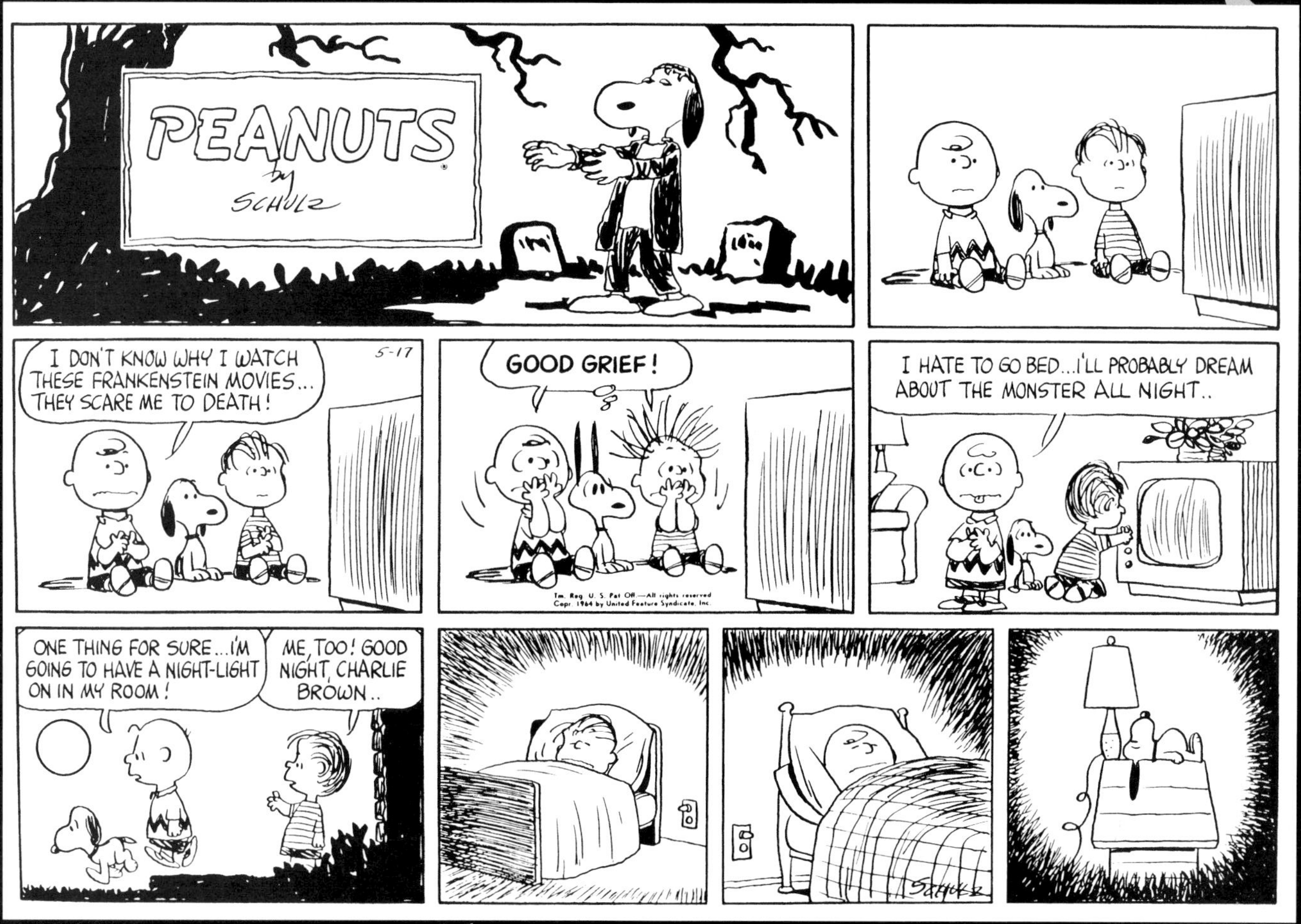
PEANUTS
by SCHULZ
5-17
I DON'T KNOW WHY I WATCH THESE FRANKENSTEIN MOVIES... THEY SCARE ME TO DEATH!
GOOD GRIEF!
Tm. Reg. U. S. Pat. Off.—All rights reserved
Copr. 1964 by United Feature Syndicate, Inc.
I HATE TO GO BED...I'LL PROBABLY DREAM ABOUT THE MONSTER ALL NIGHT..
ONE THING FOR SURE...I'M GOING TO HAVE A NIGHT-LIGHT ON IN MY ROOM!
ME, TOO! GOOD NIGHT, CHARLIE BROWN..
SCHULZ

5-17-64

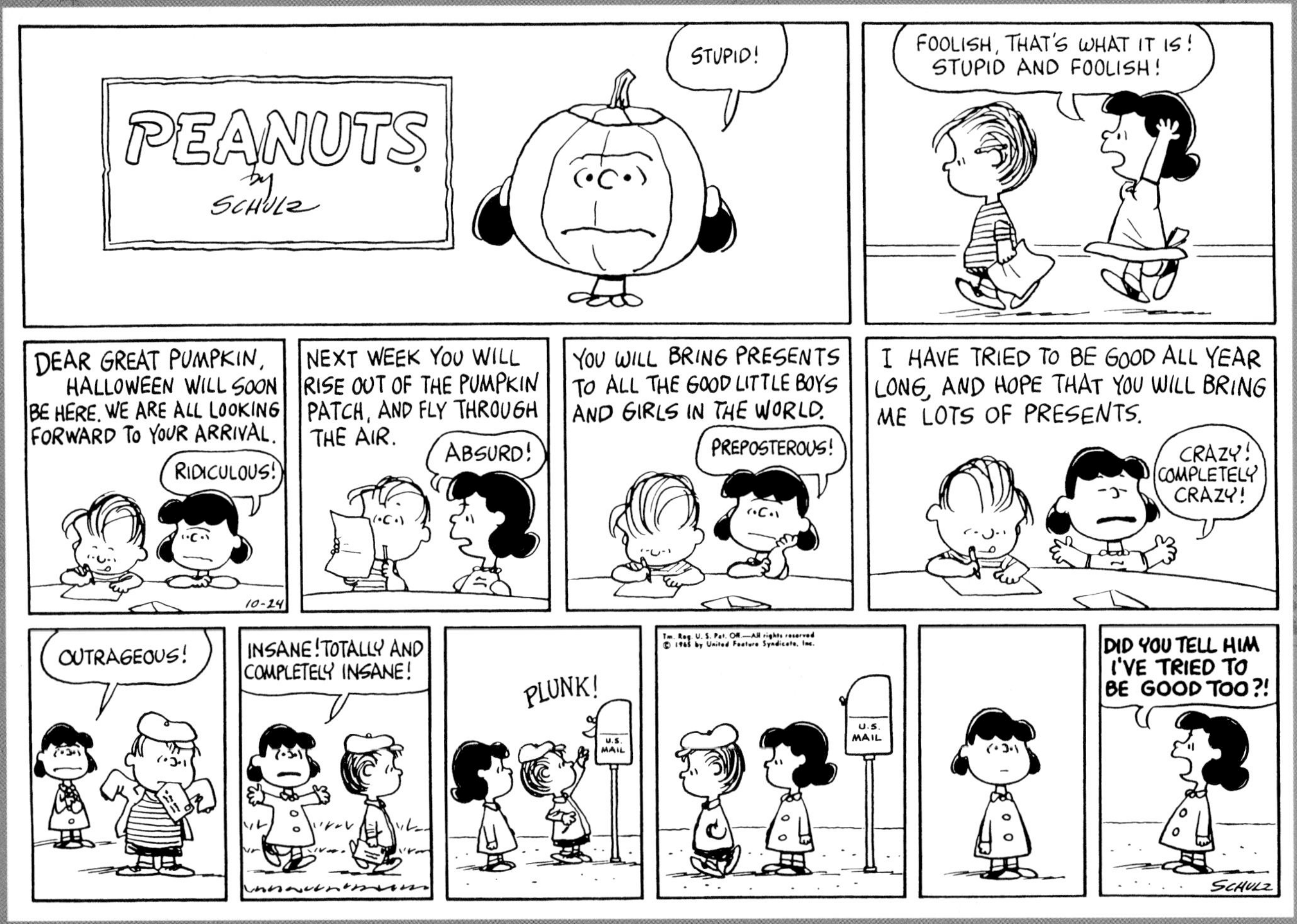
PEANUTS
by SCHULZ
STUPID!
FOOLISH, THAT'S WHAT IT IS! STUPID AND FOOLISH!
DEAR GREAT PUMPKIN, HALLOWEEN WILL SOON BE HERE. WE ARE ALL LOOKING FORWARD TO YOUR ARRIVAL.
RIDICULOUS!
10-24
NEXT WEEK YOU WILL RISE OUT OF THE PUMPKIN PATCH, AND FLY THROUGH THE AIR.
ABSURD!
YOU WILL BRING PRESENTS TO ALL THE GOOD LITTLE BOYS AND GIRLS IN THE WORLD.
PREPOSTEROUS!
I HAVE TRIED TO BE GOOD ALL YEAR LONG, AND HOPE THAT YOU WILL BRING ME LOTS OF PRESENTS.
CRAZY! COMPLETELY CRAZY!
OUTRAGEOUS!
INSANE! TOTALLY AND COMPLETELY INSANE!
PLUNK!
U.S. MAIL
Tm. Reg. U.S. Pat. Off.—All rights reserved
© 1965 by United Feature Syndicate, Inc.
U.S. MAIL
DID YOU TELL HIM I'VE TRIED TO BE GOOD TOO?!
SCHULZ

10-24-65

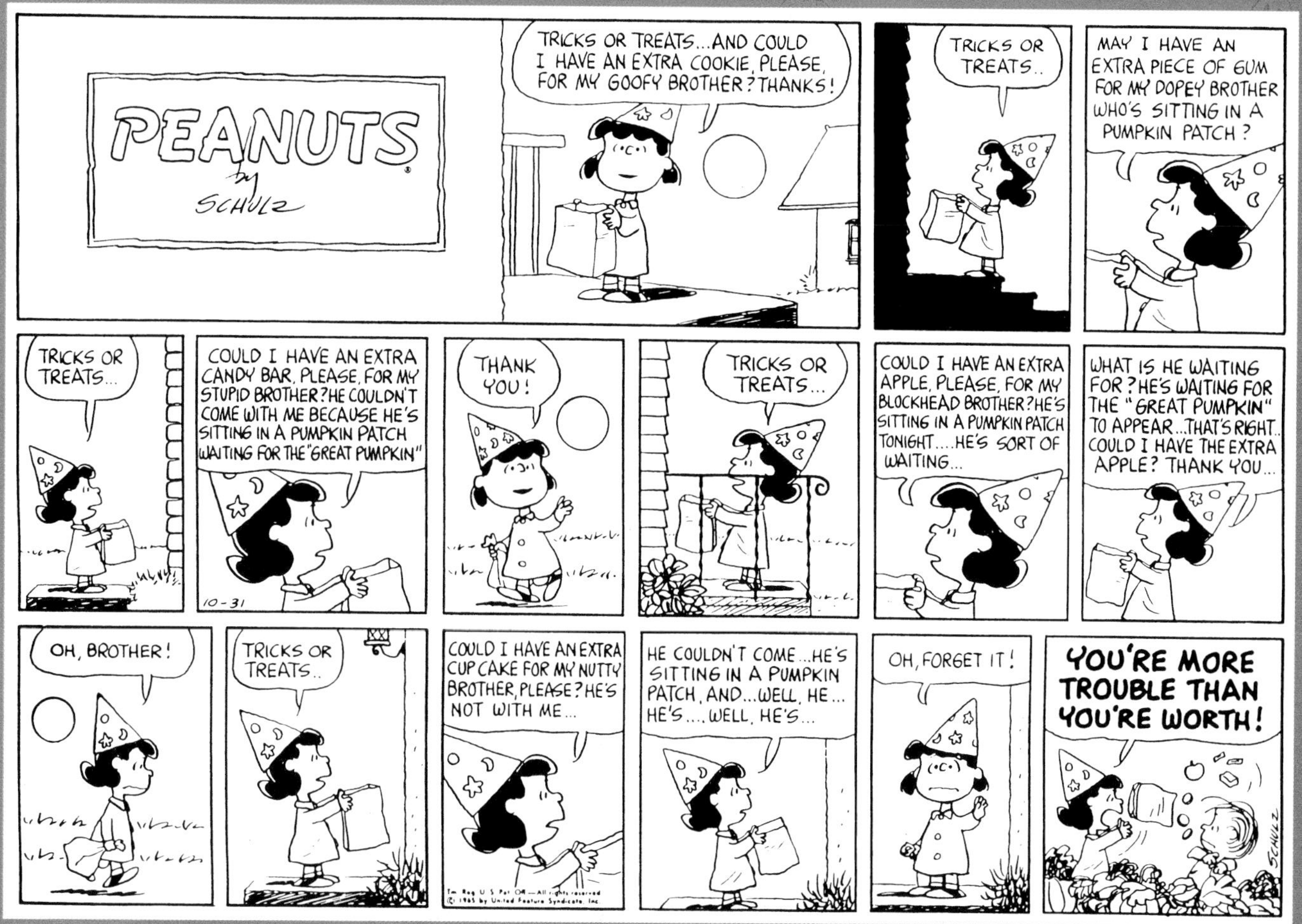
PEANUTS
by SCHULZ
TRICKS OR TREATS...AND COULD I HAVE AN EXTRA COOKIE, PLEASE, FOR MY GOOFY BROTHER? THANKS!
TRICKS OR TREATS..
MAY I HAVE AN EXTRA PIECE OF GUM FOR MY DOPEY BROTHER WHO'S SITTING IN A PUMPKIN PATCH?
TRICKS OR TREATS...
COULD I HAVE AN EXTRA CANDY BAR, PLEASE, FOR MY STUPID BROTHER? HE COULDN'T COME WITH ME BECAUSE HE'S SITTING IN A PUMPKIN PATCH WAITING FOR THE "GREAT PUMPKIN"
10-31
THANK YOU!
TRICKS OR TREATS...
COULD I HAVE AN EXTRA APPLE, PLEASE, FOR MY BLOCKHEAD BROTHER? HE'S SITTING IN A PUMPKIN PATCH TONIGHT....HE'S SORT OF WAITING...
WHAT IS HE WAITING FOR? HE'S WAITING FOR THE "GREAT PUMPKIN" TO APPEAR...THAT'S RIGHT.. COULD I HAVE THE EXTRA APPLE? THANK YOU...
OH, BROTHER!
TRICKS OR TREATS..
COULD I HAVE AN EXTRA CUP CAKE FOR MY NUTTY BROTHER, PLEASE? HE'S NOT WITH ME...
HE COULDN'T COME...HE'S SITTING IN A PUMPKIN PATCH, AND...WELL, HE... HE'S....WELL, HE'S...
OH, FORGET IT!
YOU'RE MORE TROUBLE THAN YOU'RE WORTH!
SCHULZ

10-31-65

PEANUTS
OKAY, LINUS, TELL ME ALL ABOUT THE "GREAT PUMPKIN"
WELL, IT'S LIKE THIS...
ON HALLOWEEN NIGHT, THE "GREAT PUMPKIN" CHOOSES THE PUMPKIN PATCH THAT HE THINKS IS THE MOST SINCERE... THEN HE RISES OUT OF THE PUMPKIN PATCH, AND FLIES THROUGH THE AIR BRINGING PRESENTS TO CHILDREN EVERYWHERE
10-24
I BELIEVE YOU!
YOU DO?!
FANTASTIC!
SCHULZ

10-24-66

PEANUTS
YOU KNOW WHY I BELIEVE YOUR STORY ABOUT THE "GREAT PUMPKIN"?
10-25
BECAUSE I'M VERY SUPERSTITIOUS, THAT'S WHY! THE MORE IMPOSSIBLE SOMETHING IS, THE MORE I BELIEVE IT! THAT'S THE WAY I AM!
YOU THINK THE "GREAT PUMPKIN" STORY IS IMPOSSIBLE?
OH, IT'S IMPOSSIBLE ALL RIGHT... IT'S IMPOSSIBLE, STUPID AND RIDICULOUS...
BUT I BELIEVE IT!!
SCHULZ

10-25-66

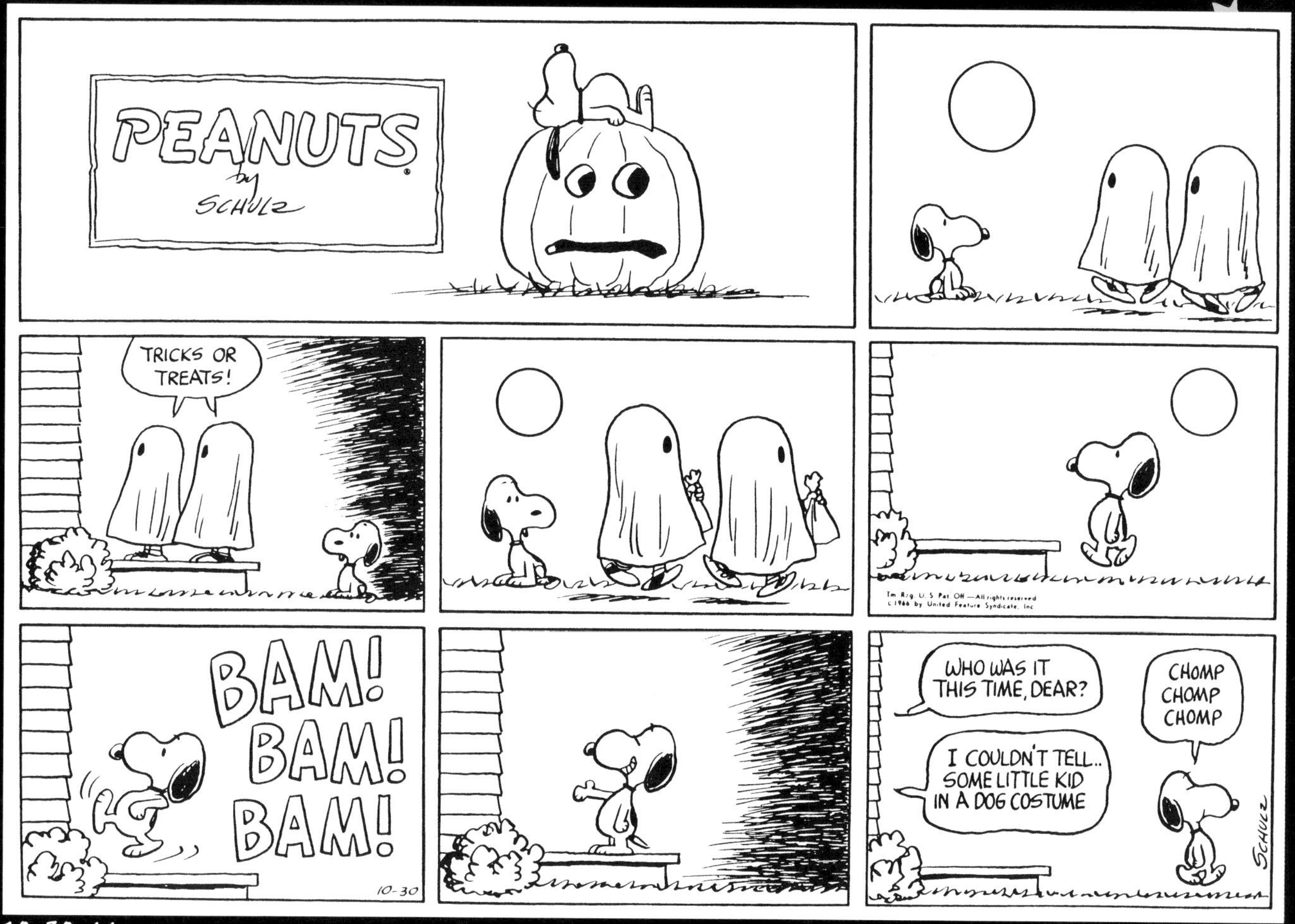
PEANUTS
by
SCHULZ
TRICKS OR TREATS!
Tm Reg. U.S. Pat. Off.—All rights reserved
©1966 by United Feature Syndicate, Inc.
BAM! BAM! BAM!
10-30
WHO WAS IT THIS TIME, DEAR?
I COULDN'T TELL.. SOME LITTLE KID IN A DOG COSTUME
CHOMP CHOMP CHOMP
SCHULZ

10-30-66

PEANUTS
I KNOW THAT THE ONLY REASON I'M SITTING OUT HERE IS BECAUSE I'M SUPERSTITIOUS..
WHY ELSE WOULD I SIT IN A PUMPKIN PATCH ALL NIGHT WAITING FOR THE "GREAT PUMPKIN"?
Tm. Reg. U. S. Pat. Off.—All rights reserved ©1966 by United Feature Syndicate, Inc.
10/31
OF COURSE, I'M THE TRUSTING TYPE, TOO... I'M TRUSTING AND FAITHFUL AND SUPERSTITIOUS...
LET'S FACE IT... I'M ALSO A LITTLE BIT STUPID!
SCHULZ

10-31-66

PEANUTS
SNOOPY, I HAVE GREAT NEWS FOR YOU...
Tm. Reg. U. S. Pat. Off.—All rights reserved ©1967 by United Feature Syndicate, Inc.
I AM GOING TO LET YOU SIT IN THE PUMPKIN PATCH WITH ME THIS YEAR, AND WAIT FOR THE ARRIVAL OF THE "GREAT PUMPKIN"!
HMM...TO QUOTE A WELL-WORN AND TIME-HONORED PHRASE...
10-25
"THRILLSVILLE!"
SCHULZ

10-25-67

PEANUTS

ON HALLOWEEN NIGHT THE "GREAT PUMPKIN" RISES OUT OF THE PUMPKIN PATCH THAT HE PICKS AS THE MOST SINCERE

THEN HE FLIES THROUGH THE AIR BRINGING TOYS TO ALL THE GOOD CHILDREN IN THE WORLD!

JUST THINK, SNOOPY, IF HE PICKS THIS PUMPKIN PATCH, YOU AND I WILL BE HERE TO SEE HIM!

FRANKLY, THIS LOOKS LIKE A GOOD PLACE TO GET MUGGED!

10-26-67

PEANUTS

I WISH YOU COULD TALK, SNOOPY...

HERE YOU ARE SITTING IN A PUMPKIN PATCH WITH THE POSSIBILITY OF SEEING THE "GREAT PUMPKIN"... IT'S AN EMOTIONAL EXPERIENCE..

I'D REALLY BE INTERESTED IN KNOWING WHAT THOUGHTS ARE RUNNING THROUGH YOUR MIND...

WHEN DO WE EAT?

10-27-67

PEANUTS
WHAT ARE YOU GUYS DOING?
WE'RE WAITING FOR THE "GREAT PUMPKIN"
IF HE SELECTS THIS PUMPKIN PATCH AS THE MOST SINCERE, WE'LL GET TO SEE HIM!
OH, BROTHER..
I THINK YOU'RE BOTH CRAZY!
WE DON'T CARE WHAT YOU THINK, DO WE, SNOOPY?
Tm. Reg. U. S. Pat. Off.—All rights reserved
©1967 by United Feature Syndicate, Inc.
SCHULZ 10-28

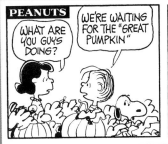

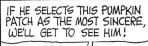

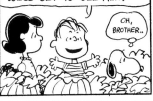

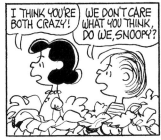

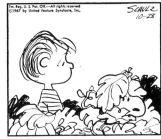

10-28-67

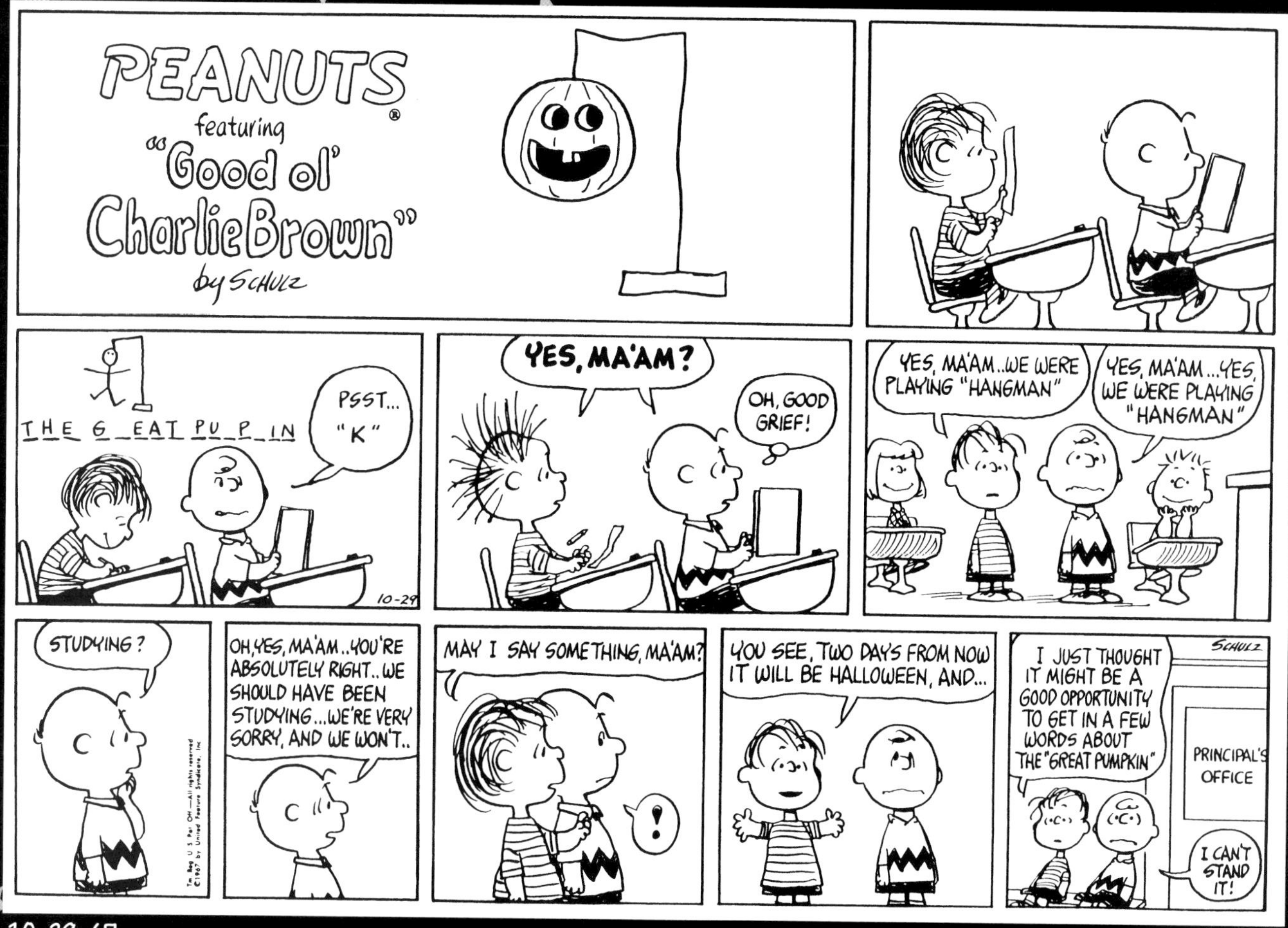
PEANUTS®
featuring
"Good ol' Charlie Brown"
by SCHULZ
THE G_EAT PU_P_IN
PSST... "K"
10-29
YES, MA'AM?
OH, GOOD GRIEF!
YES, MA'AM..WE WERE PLAYING "HANGMAN"
YES, MA'AM...YES, WE WERE PLAYING "HANGMAN"
STUDYING?
Tm Reg U S Pat Off—All rights reserved ©1967 by United Feature Syndicate, Inc
OH, YES, MA'AM..YOU'RE ABSOLUTELY RIGHT..WE SHOULD HAVE BEEN STUDYING...WE'RE VERY SORRY, AND WE WON'T..
MAY I SAY SOMETHING, MA'AM?
!
YOU SEE, TWO DAYS FROM NOW IT WILL BE HALLOWEEN, AND...
SCHULZ
I JUST THOUGHT IT MIGHT BE A GOOD OPPORTUNITY TO GET IN A FEW WORDS ABOUT THE "GREAT PUMPKIN"
PRINCIPAL'S OFFICE
I CAN'T STAND IT!

10-29-67

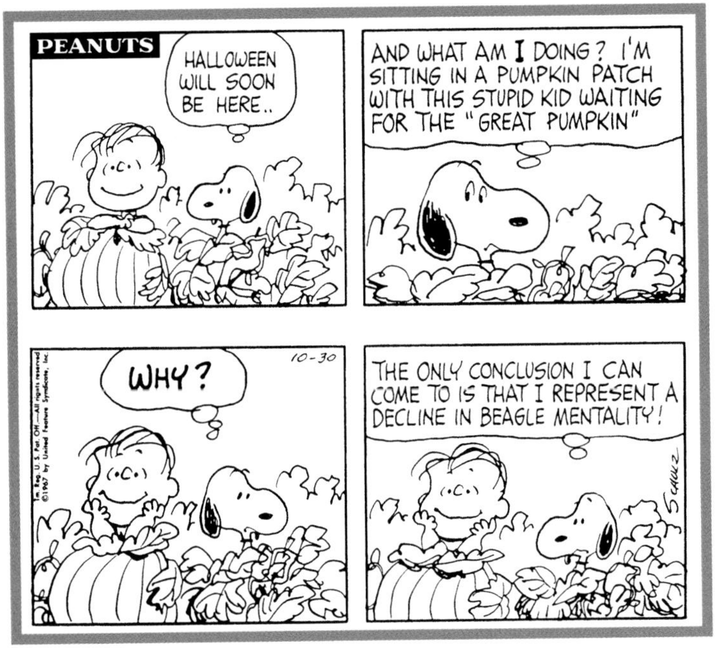
PEANUTS
HALLOWEEN WILL SOON BE HERE..
AND WHAT AM I DOING? I'M SITTING IN A PUMPKIN PATCH WITH THIS STUPID KID WAITING FOR THE "GREAT PUMPKIN"
10-30
WHY?
Tm. Reg. U. S. Pat. Off.—All rights reserved
©1967 by United Feature Syndicate, Inc.
THE ONLY CONCLUSION I CAN COME TO IS THAT I REPRESENT A DECLINE IN BEAGLE MENTALITY!
SCHULZ

10-30-67

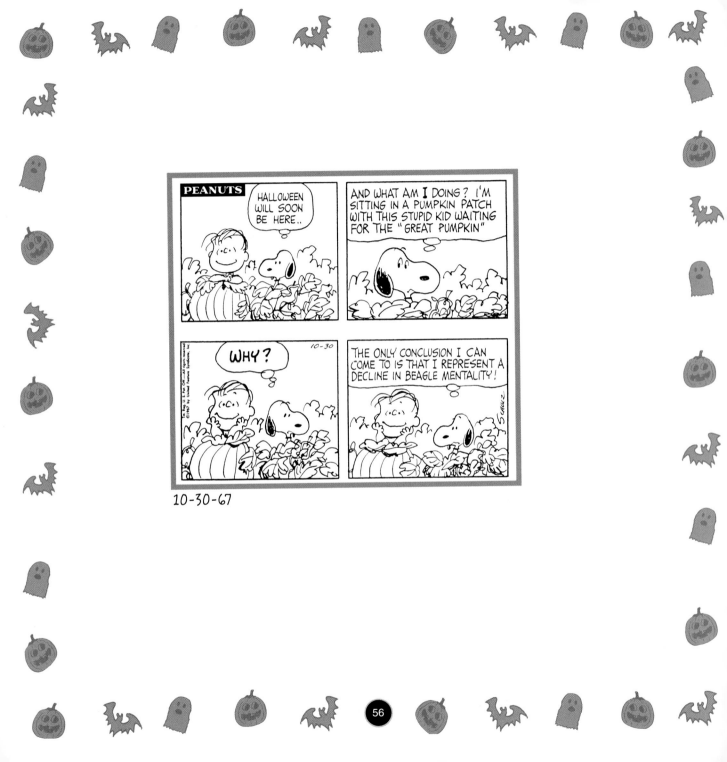

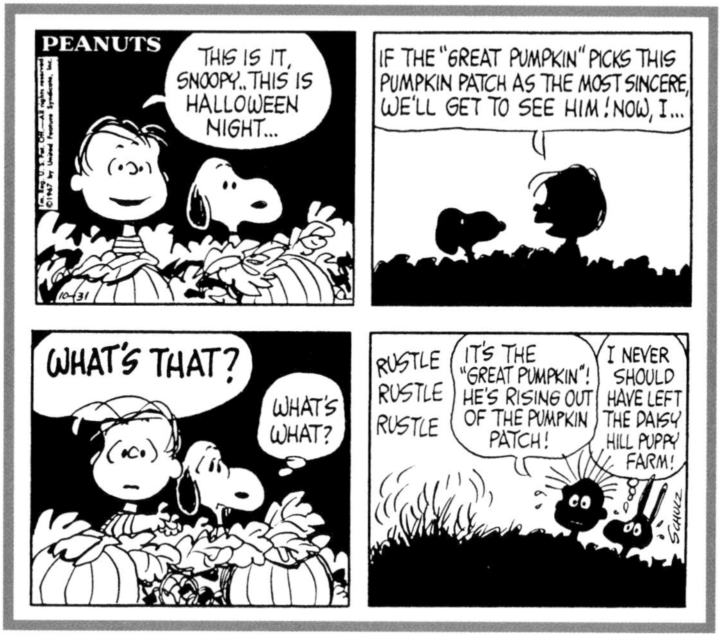
PEANUTS
THIS IS IT, SNOOPY.. THIS IS HALLOWEEN NIGHT...
IF THE "GREAT PUMPKIN" PICKS THIS PUMPKIN PATCH AS THE MOST SINCERE, WE'LL GET TO SEE HIM! NOW, I...
WHAT'S THAT?
WHAT'S WHAT?
RUSTLE RUSTLE RUSTLE
IT'S THE "GREAT PUMPKIN"! HE'S RISING OUT OF THE PUMPKIN PATCH!
I NEVER SHOULD HAVE LEFT THE DAISY HILL PUPPY FARM!
SCHULZ

10-31-67

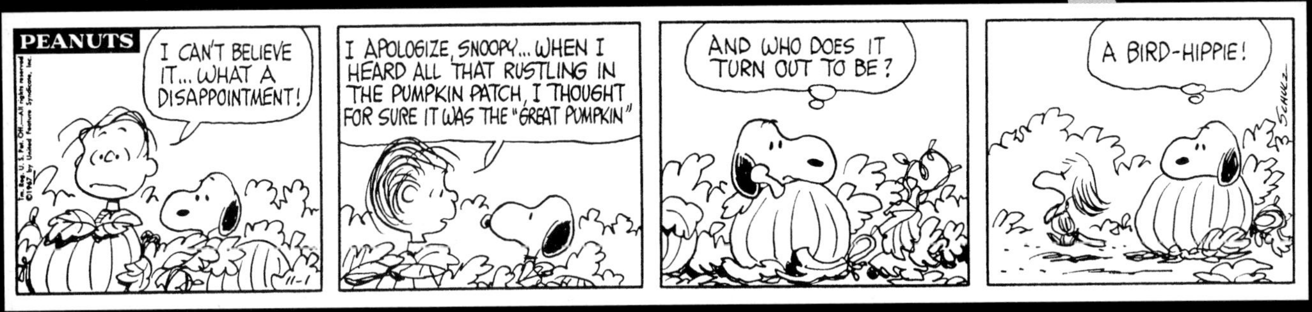
PEANUTS
I CAN'T BELIEVE IT... WHAT A DISAPPOINTMENT!
I APOLOGIZE, SNOOPY... WHEN I HEARD ALL THAT RUSTLING IN THE PUMPKIN PATCH, I THOUGHT FOR SURE IT WAS THE "GREAT PUMPKIN"
AND WHO DOES IT TURN OUT TO BE?
A BIRD-HIPPIE!
SCHULZ

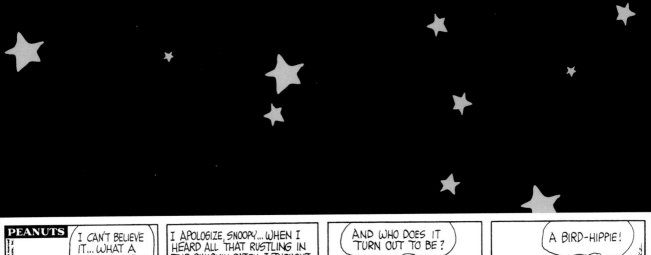

11-1-67

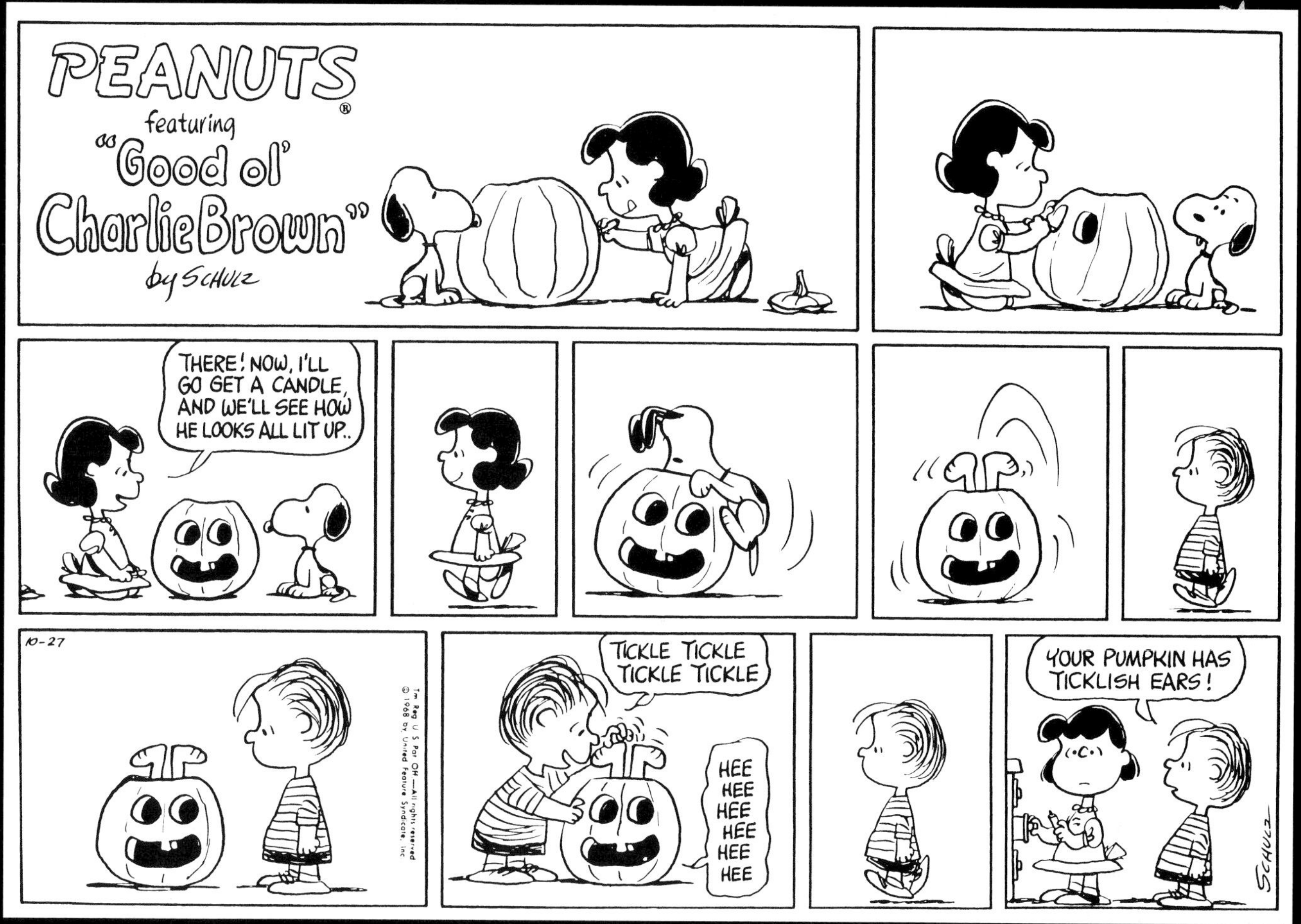
PEANUTS
featuring
"Good ol' Charlie Brown"
by SCHULZ
THERE! NOW, I'LL GO GET A CANDLE, AND WE'LL SEE HOW HE LOOKS ALL LIT UP..
10-27
Tm Reg U S Pat Off —All rights reserved
© 1968 by United Feature Syndicate, Inc
TICKLE TICKLE TICKLE TICKLE
HEE HEE HEE HEE HEE HEE
YOUR PUMPKIN HAS TICKLISH EARS!
SCHULZ

10-27-68

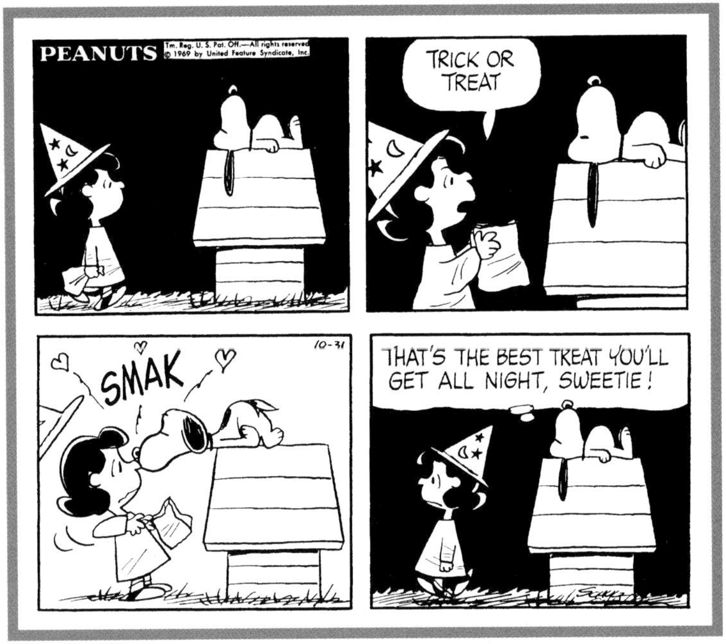
PEANUTS
Tm. Reg. U. S. Pat. Off.—All rights reserved
© 1969 by United Feature Syndicate, Inc.
TRICK OR TREAT
SMAK
10-31
THAT'S THE BEST TREAT YOU'LL GET ALL NIGHT, SWEETIE!

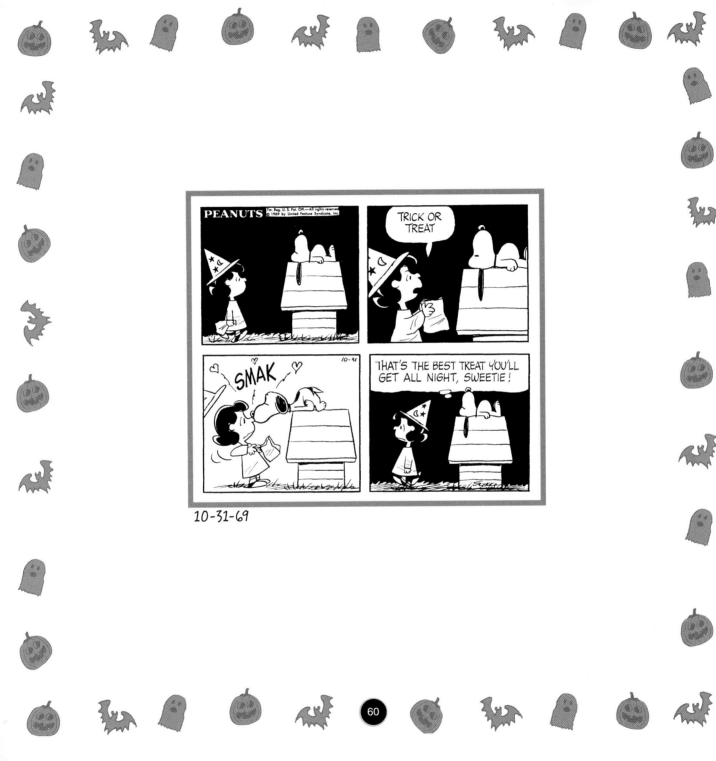

10-31-69

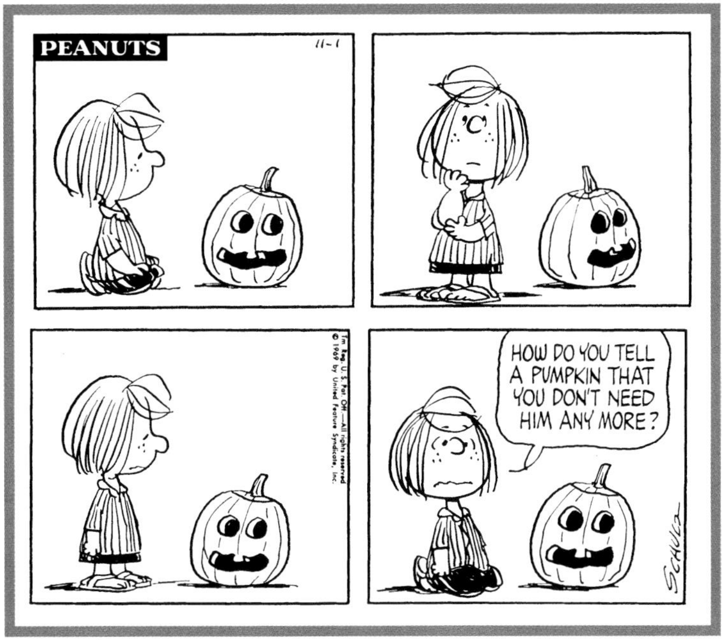
PEANUTS
11-1
Tm Reg. U.S. Pat. Off.—All rights reserved © 1969 by United Feature Syndicate, Inc.
HOW DO YOU TELL A PUMPKIN THAT YOU DON'T NEED HIM ANY MORE?
SCHULZ

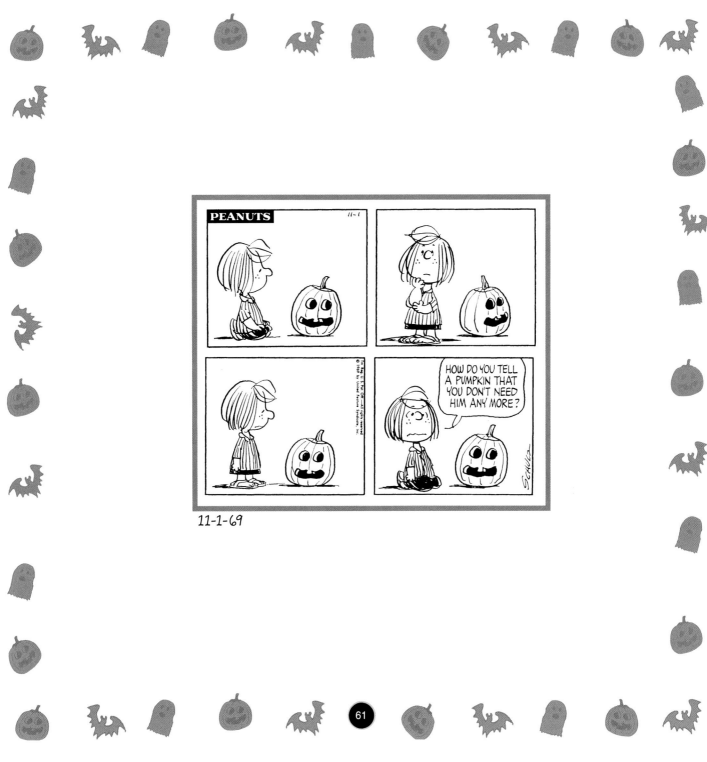

11-1-69

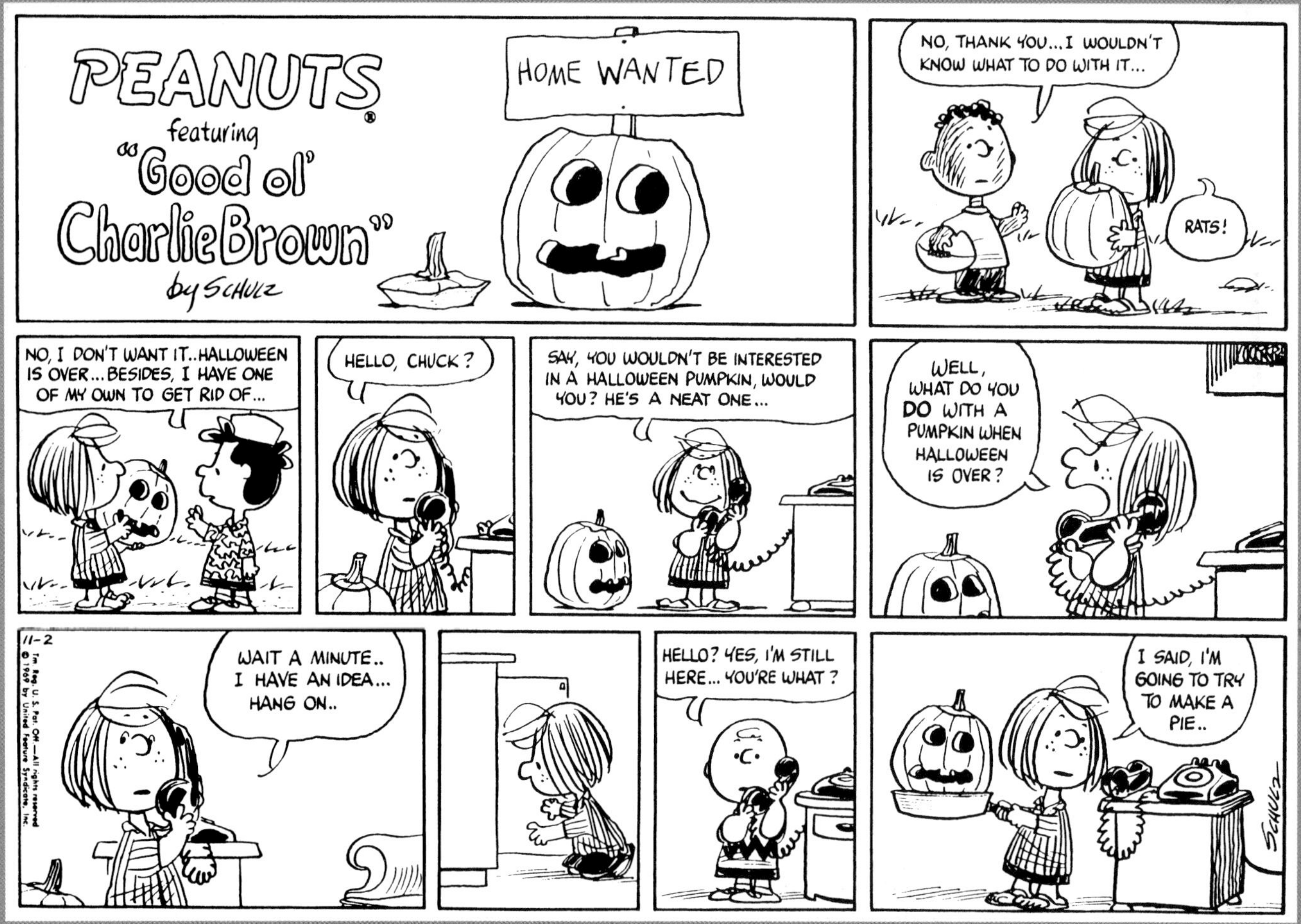
PEANUTS®
featuring "Good ol' CharlieBrown"
by SCHULZ
HOME WANTED
NO, THANK YOU... I WOULDN'T KNOW WHAT TO DO WITH IT...
RATS!
NO, I DON'T WANT IT..HALLOWEEN IS OVER... BESIDES, I HAVE ONE OF MY OWN TO GET RID OF...
HELLO, CHUCK?
SAY, YOU WOULDN'T BE INTERESTED IN A HALLOWEEN PUMPKIN, WOULD YOU? HE'S A NEAT ONE...
WELL, WHAT DO YOU DO WITH A PUMPKIN WHEN HALLOWEEN IS OVER?
11-2
Tm Reg. U. S. Pat. Off.—All rights reserved © 1969 by United Feature Syndicate, Inc.
WAIT A MINUTE.. I HAVE AN IDEA... HANG ON..
HELLO? YES, I'M STILL HERE... YOU'RE WHAT?
I SAID, I'M GOING TO TRY TO MAKE A PIE..
SCHULZ

11-2-69

PEANUTS
Z
ONE OF US ALWAYS STAYS AWAKE IN CASE OF VAMPIRES
SCHULZ

5-6-70

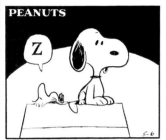

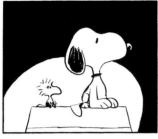

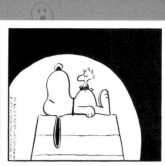

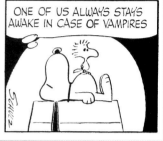

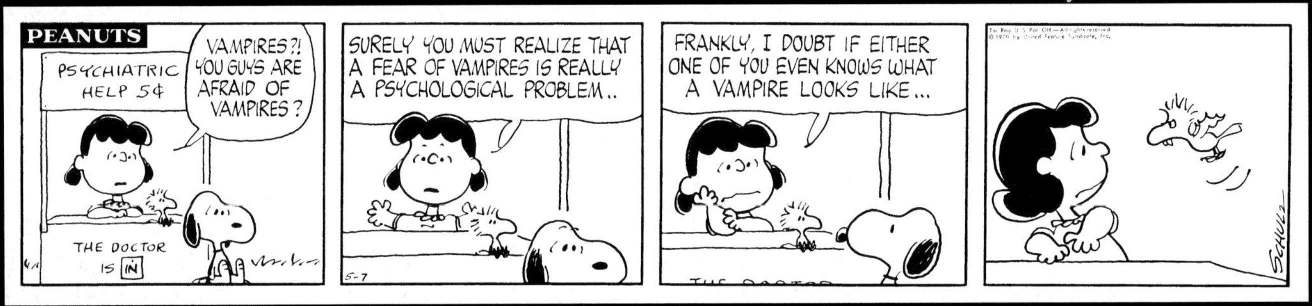
PEANUTS
PSYCHIATRIC HELP 5¢
VAMPIRES?! YOU GUYS ARE AFRAID OF VAMPIRES?
THE DOCTOR IS IN
SURELY YOU MUST REALIZE THAT A FEAR OF VAMPIRES IS REALLY A PSYCHOLOGICAL PROBLEM..
FRANKLY, I DOUBT IF EITHER ONE OF YOU EVEN KNOWS WHAT A VAMPIRE LOOKS LIKE...
SCHULZ

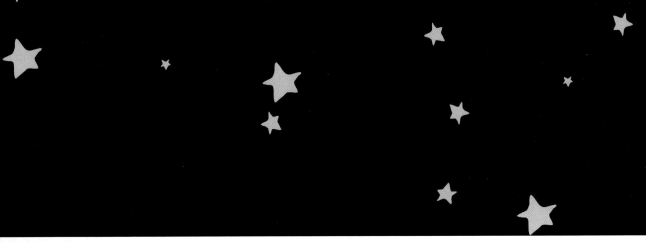

5-7-70

PEANUTS
THIS IS NOT A GOOD PLACE TO BE IF A VAMPIRE COMES AROUND
I THINK WE'RE SAFER IN HERE, DOWNSTAIRS, IN THE LIBRARY...
UNDER THE POOL TABLE!
5-8
SCHULZ

5-8-70

PEANUTS
IT WAS MIDNIGHT.. SHE TURNED TO THE BEDROOM WINDOW... SUDDENLY, SHE SAW A VAMPIRE!
PEPPERMINT PATTY! YOU'RE THE ONE WHO'S BEEN SCARING THEM WITH THOSE VAMPIRE STORIES! YOU OUGHT TO BE ASHAMED!!
JUST A LITTLE HARMLESS FUN, CHUCK...THEY DON'T REALLY BELIEVE THOSE STORIES, DO YOU, SNOOPY?
5-9
SCHULZ

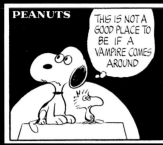

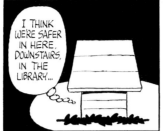

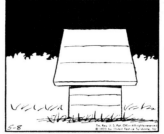

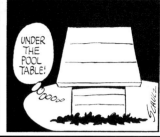

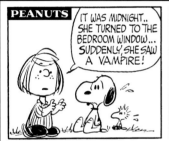

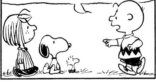

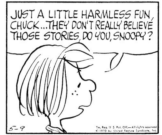

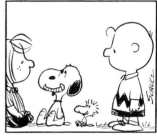

5-9-70

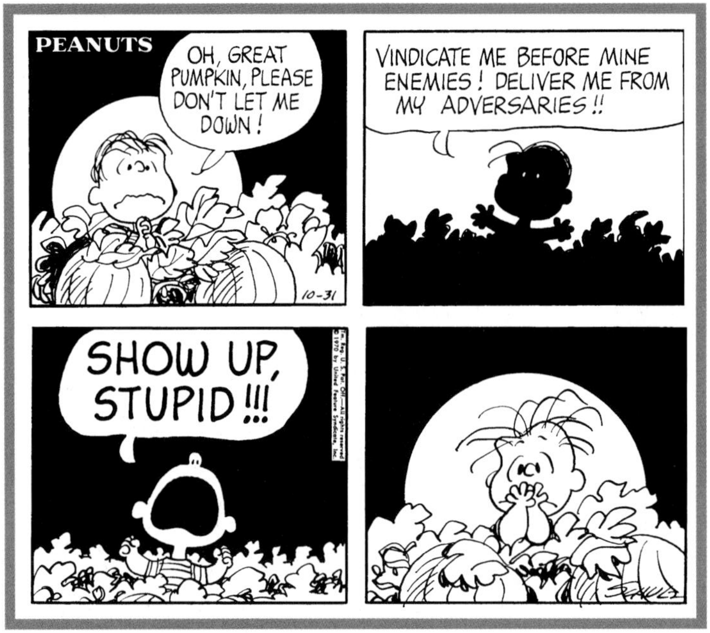
PEANUTS
OH, GREAT PUMPKIN, PLEASE DON'T LET ME DOWN!
10-31
VINDICATE ME BEFORE MINE ENEMIES! DELIVER ME FROM MY ADVERSARIES!!
SHOW UP, STUPID!!!

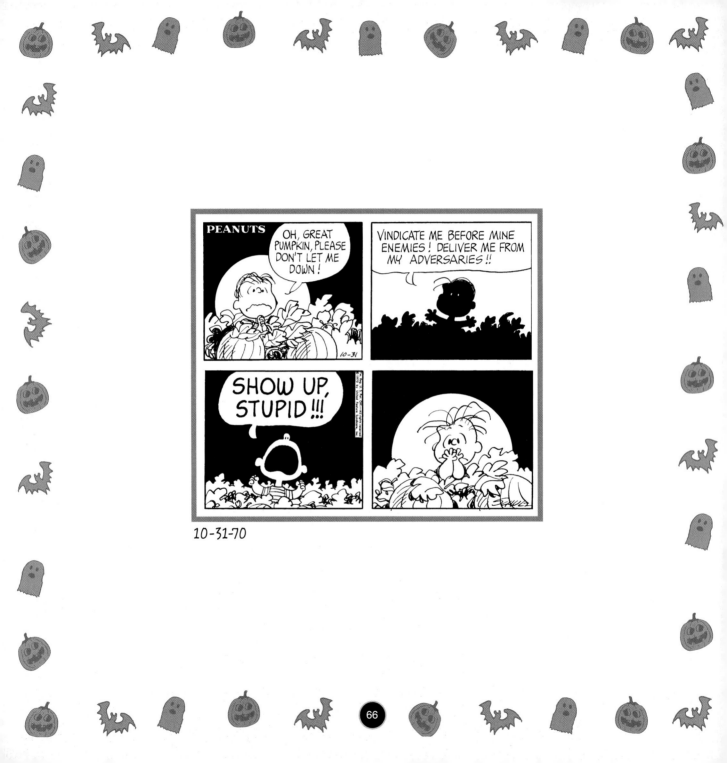

10-31-70

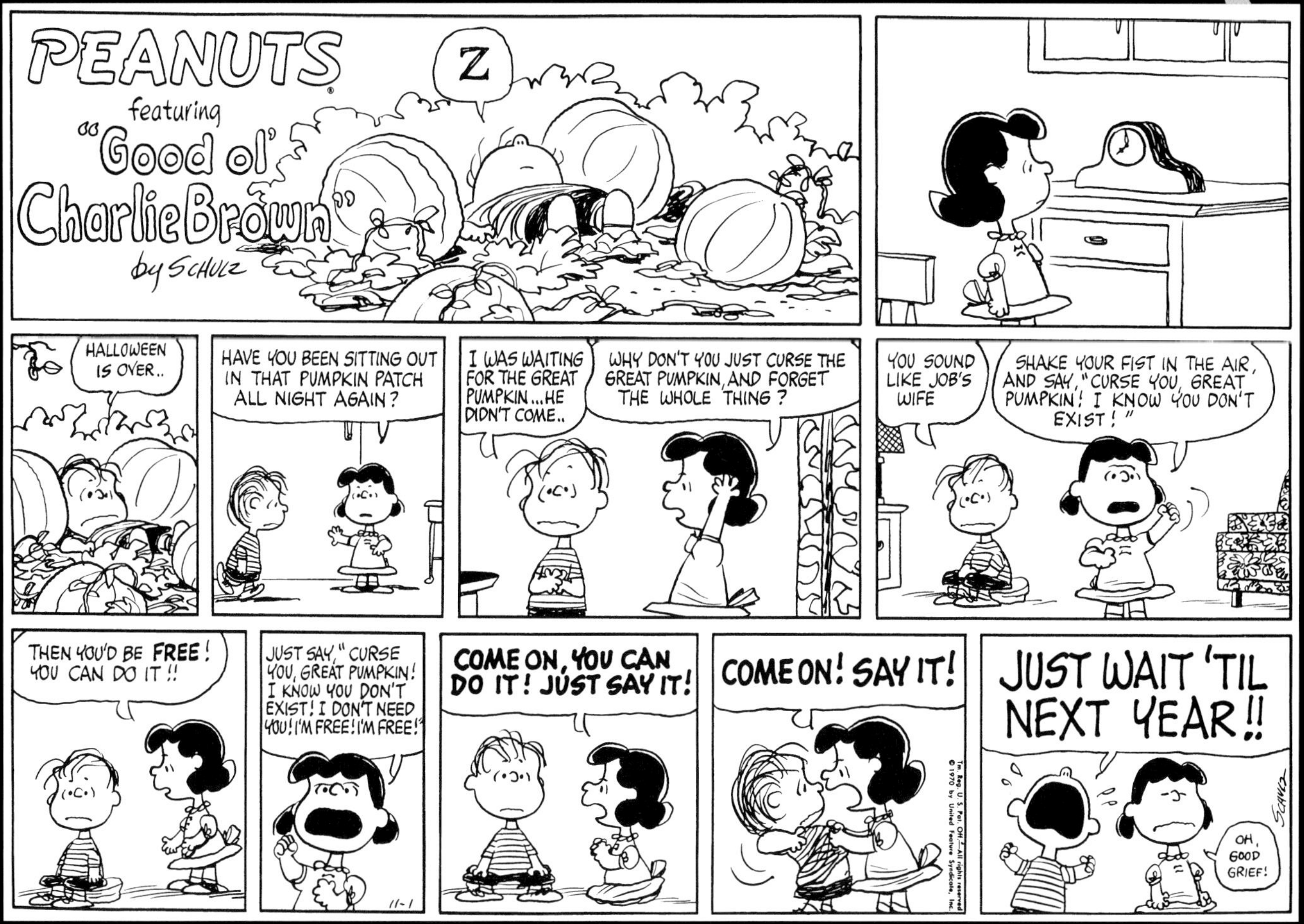
PEANUTS
featuring "Good ol' Charlie Brown"
by SCHULZ
Z
HALLOWEEN IS OVER..
HAVE YOU BEEN SITTING OUT IN THAT PUMPKIN PATCH ALL NIGHT AGAIN?
I WAS WAITING FOR THE GREAT PUMPKIN...HE DIDN'T COME..
WHY DON'T YOU JUST CURSE THE GREAT PUMPKIN, AND FORGET THE WHOLE THING?
YOU SOUND LIKE JOB'S WIFE
SHAKE YOUR FIST IN THE AIR, AND SAY, "CURSE YOU, GREAT PUMPKIN! I KNOW YOU DON'T EXIST!"
THEN YOU'D BE FREE! YOU CAN DO IT!!
JUST SAY, "CURSE YOU, GREAT PUMPKIN! I KNOW YOU DON'T EXIST! I DON'T NEED YOU! I'M FREE! I'M FREE!"
11-1
COME ON, YOU CAN DO IT! JUST SAY IT!
COME ON! SAY IT!
Tm. Reg. U.S. Pat. Off.—All rights reserved © 1970 by United Feature Syndicate, Inc.
JUST WAIT 'TIL NEXT YEAR!!
OH, GOOD GRIEF!
SCHULZ

11-1-70

PEANUTS
IS THIS MOVIE THE ONE ABOUT GIANT SPIDERS, GREEN RATS AND PURPLE VAMPIRES?
SHE SAYS, NO... THIS IS THE ONE ABOUT SHRUNKEN HEADS, WOOLLY WEREWOLVES AND THREE-HEADED MARS-MEN..
LET'S WAIT
WE'RE GOING TO WAIT, THANK YOU... WE WANTED TO SEE THE ONE ABOUT THE GIANT SPIDERS, GREEN RATS AND PURPLE VAMPIRES..
DON'T FEEL GUILTY.. THERE'S NOTHING WRONG WITH BEING CHOOSY...
SCHULZ
Tm. Reg. U.S. Pat. Off.—All rights reserved © 1971 by United Feature Syndicate, Inc.
9-21

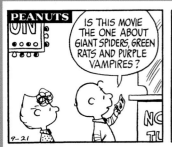

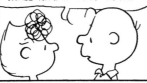

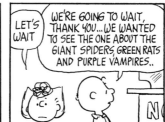

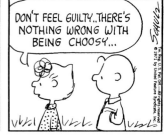

9-21-71

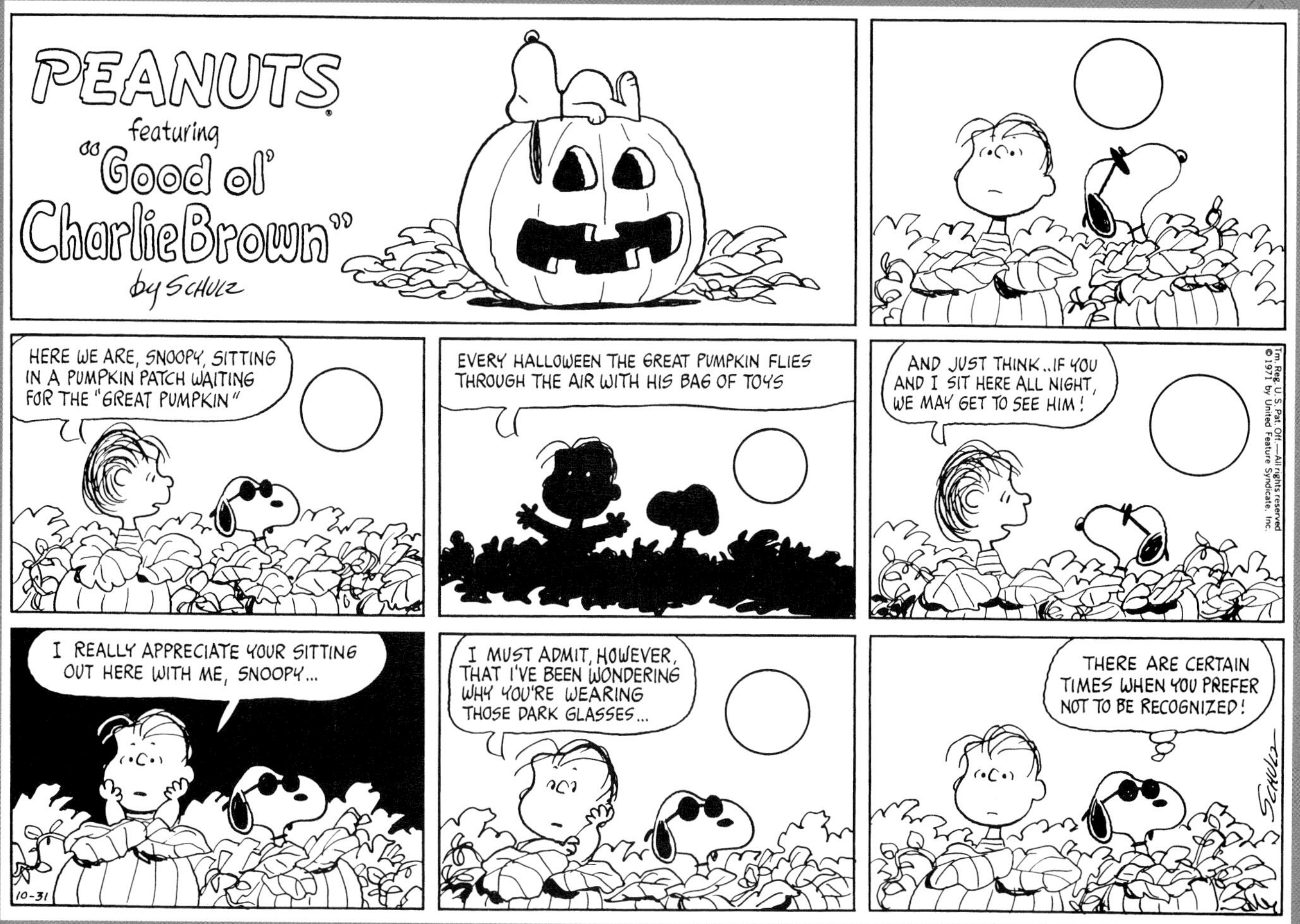
PEANUTS
featuring
"Good ol' CharlieBrown"
by SCHULZ
HERE WE ARE, SNOOPY, SITTING IN A PUMPKIN PATCH WAITING FOR THE "GREAT PUMPKIN"
EVERY HALLOWEEN THE GREAT PUMPKIN FLIES THROUGH THE AIR WITH HIS BAG OF TOYS
AND JUST THINK..IF YOU AND I SIT HERE ALL NIGHT, WE MAY GET TO SEE HIM!
Tm. Reg. U.S. Pat. Off.—All rights reserved
© 1971 by United Feature Syndicate, Inc.
I REALLY APPRECIATE YOUR SITTING OUT HERE WITH ME, SNOOPY...
I MUST ADMIT, HOWEVER, THAT I'VE BEEN WONDERING WHY YOU'RE WEARING THOSE DARK GLASSES...
THERE ARE CERTAIN TIMES WHEN YOU PREFER NOT TO BE RECOGNIZED!
10-31
SCHULZ

10-31-71

PEANUTS
THIS IS WHAT HAPPENS ON HALLOWEEN NIGHT, MARCIE...
THE GREAT PUMPKIN RISES OUT OF THE PUMPKIN PATCH, AND FLIES THROUGH THE AIR AND BRINGS TOYS TO ALL THE CHILDREN IN THE WORLD!
10-29
Tm. Reg. U. S. Pat. Off.—All rights reserved
© 1973 by United Feature Syndicate, Inc.
I'VE HEARD ABOUT YOU
SCHULZ

10-29-73

PEANUTS
SIR, DO YOU BELIEVE IN THE GREAT PUMPKIN?
THE GREAT WHAT?
10-30
LINUS SAYS THERE'S A GREAT PUMPKIN WHO BRINGS US TOYS ON HALLOWEEN NIGHT
Tm. Reg. U. S. Pat. Off.—All rights reserved
© 1973 by United Feature Syndicate, Inc.
THE WORLD IS FILLED WITH WEIRD PEOPLE, MARCIE...
I'M FINDING THAT OUT, SIR!
SCHULZ

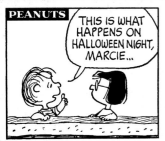

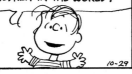

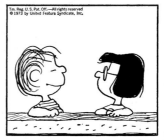

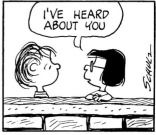

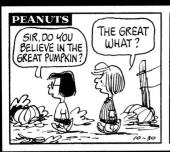

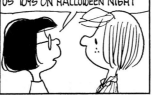

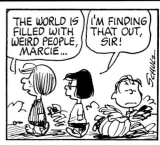

10-30-73

PEANUTS
OH, GREAT PUMPKIN, WHY HAST THOU CAST ME OFF?
HOW LONG, OH, GREAT PUMPKIN, WILT THOU HIDE THYSELF FROM ME?
Tm. Reg. U.S. Pat. Off.—All rights reserved
© 1973 by United Feature Syndicate, Inc.
MINE ENEMIES REPROACH ME ALL THE DAY! BRING THOU ME OUT OF MY DISTRESS!
RATS!
SCHULZ

10-31-73

PEANUTS
MAY I ASK YOU SOMETHING?
IT'S ABOUT LAST NIGHT...
DID THE GREAT SQUASH EVER SHOW UP?
Tm. Reg. U.S. Pat. Off.—All rights reserved
© 1973 by United Feature Syndicate, Inc.
THAT'S PUMPKIN!!!
SCHULZ

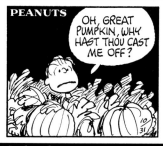

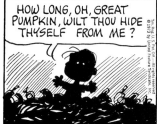

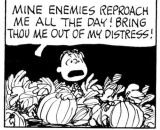

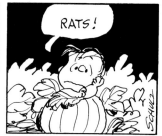

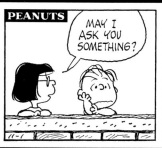

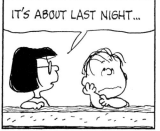

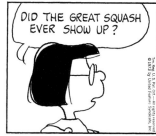

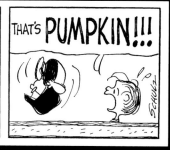

11-1-73

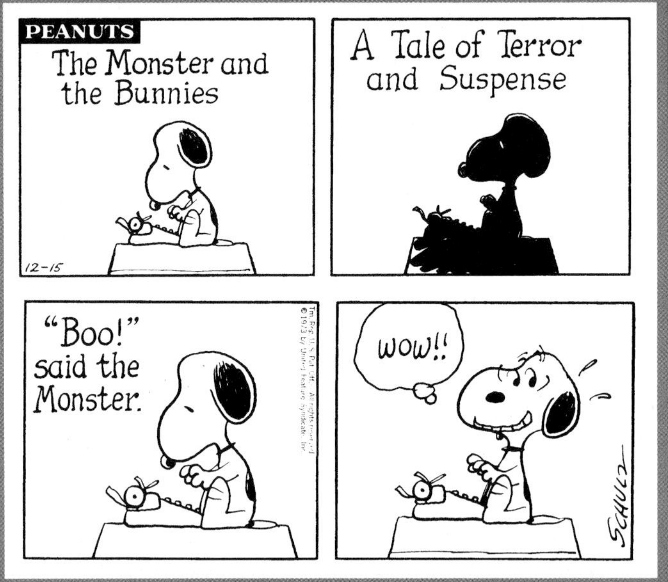
PEANUTS
The Monster and the Bunnies
12-15
A Tale of Terror and Suspense
"Boo!" said the Monster.
WOW!!
SCHULZ

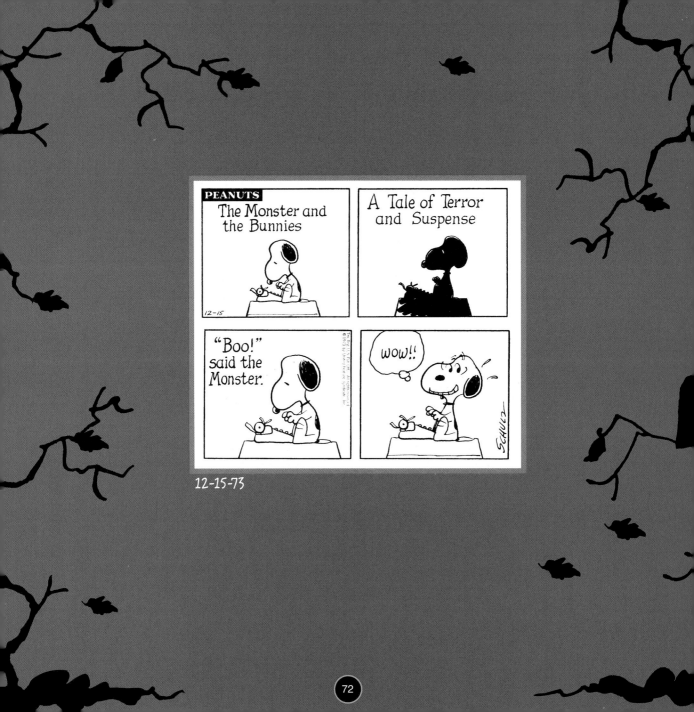

12-15-73

10 GREAT WRITERS OF SPOOKY STORIES

Bram Stoker
Mary Shelley
Edgar Allan Poe
Stephen King
R. L. Stine
Ray Bradbury
H. P. Lovecraft
Robert Louis Stevenson
Arthur Conan Doyle
Literary Ace Snoopy

Jiggle Pumpkins and Wiggle Bats

- 1 box orange Jell-O™
- 1 box blackberry or grape Jell-O™

Pearl B. Wait, who introduced Jell-O™ to the American public in 1897, must have been a fun person. Not only do these pumpkins and bats jiggle and wiggle, they're fruity good, too. Your kids will have a blast making and eating these, and, I dare say, should you have the gumption to serve them at a dinner party, your guest will go batty (sorry!) for them, too.

Lightly spray 2 shallow pans, such as jelly roll pans, with nonstick cooking spray.

Prepare the boxes of Jell-O™ according to the package directions. Pour each into a prepared pan and chill until set.

Using cookie cutters, cut pumpkins from the orange Jell-O™ and bats from the purple Jell-O™. Eat!

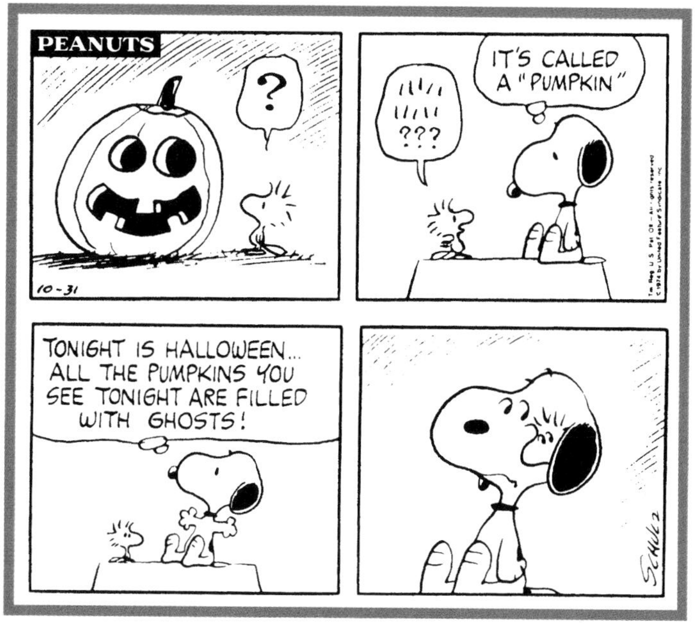
PEANUTS
?
IT'S CALLED A "PUMPKIN"
???
TONIGHT IS HALLOWEEN... ALL THE PUMPKINS YOU SEE TONIGHT ARE FILLED WITH GHOSTS!
SCHULZ

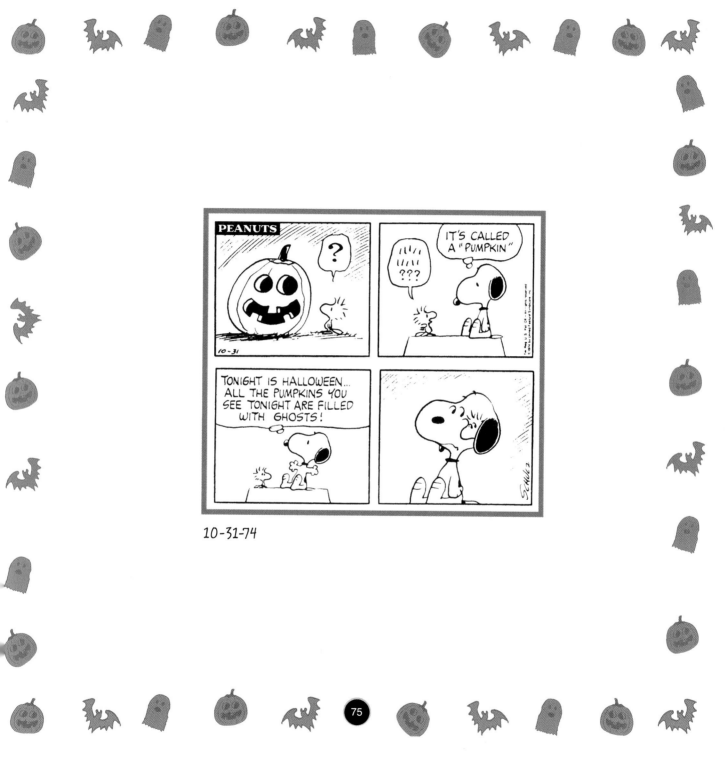

10-31-74

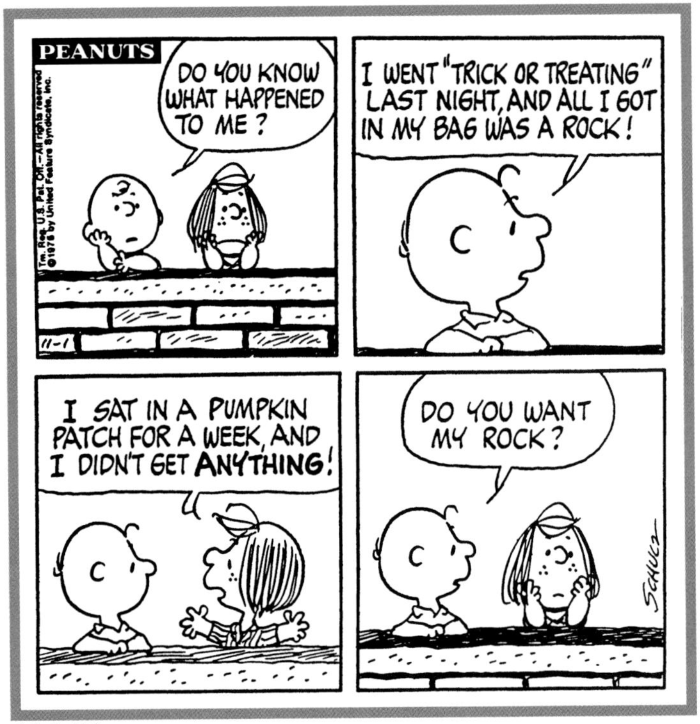
PEANUTS
Tm. Reg. U.S. Pat. Off.—All rights reserved
©1975 by United Feature Syndicate, Inc.
DO YOU KNOW WHAT HAPPENED TO ME?
11-1
I WENT "TRICK OR TREATING" LAST NIGHT, AND ALL I GOT IN MY BAG WAS A ROCK!
I SAT IN A PUMPKIN PATCH FOR A WEEK, AND I DIDN'T GET **ANYTHING**!
DO YOU WANT MY ROCK?
SCHULZ

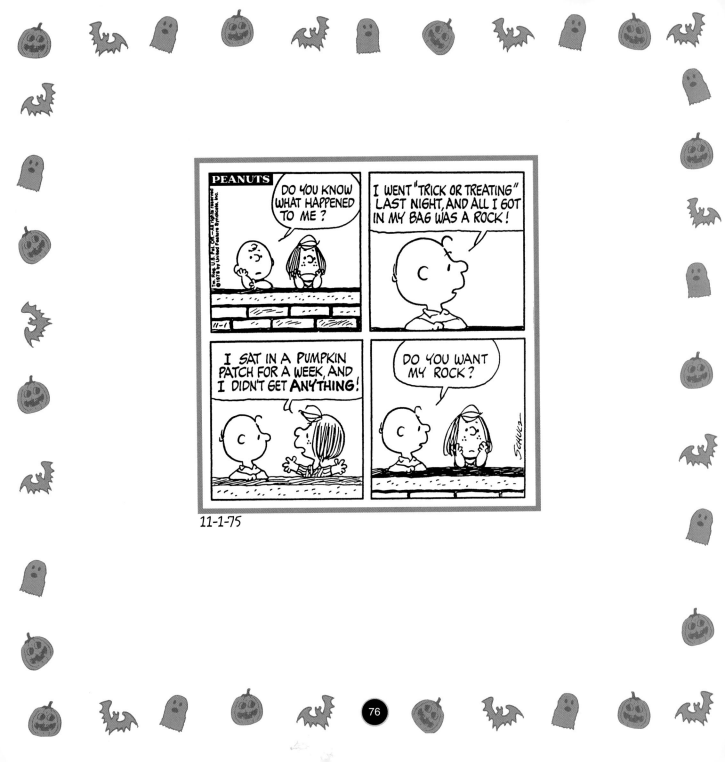

11-1-75

Peppermint Patty Brownies

Mix margarine, sugar, and vanilla. Beat in eggs till well blended. Stir in flour, cocoa, baking powder, and salt. Blend well.

Reserve 2 cups of batter (set aside).

Grease a 13 x 9 x 2-inch pan. Spread remaining batter in prepared pan. Arrange peppermint patties in a single layer over batter, about 1/2 inch apart.

Spread reserved 2 cups batter over patties. Bake at 350°F for 50 to 55 minutes till brownies begin to pull away from the sides of the pan. Cool completely in pan on wire rack.

Makes 12 servings.

- 1 ½ cups margarine
- 3 cups sugar
- 1 tablespoon vanilla extract
- 5 eggs
- 2 cups all purpose flour
- 1 cup unsweetened cocoa powder
- 1 teaspoon baking powder
- 1 teaspoon salt
- 24 small peppermint patties

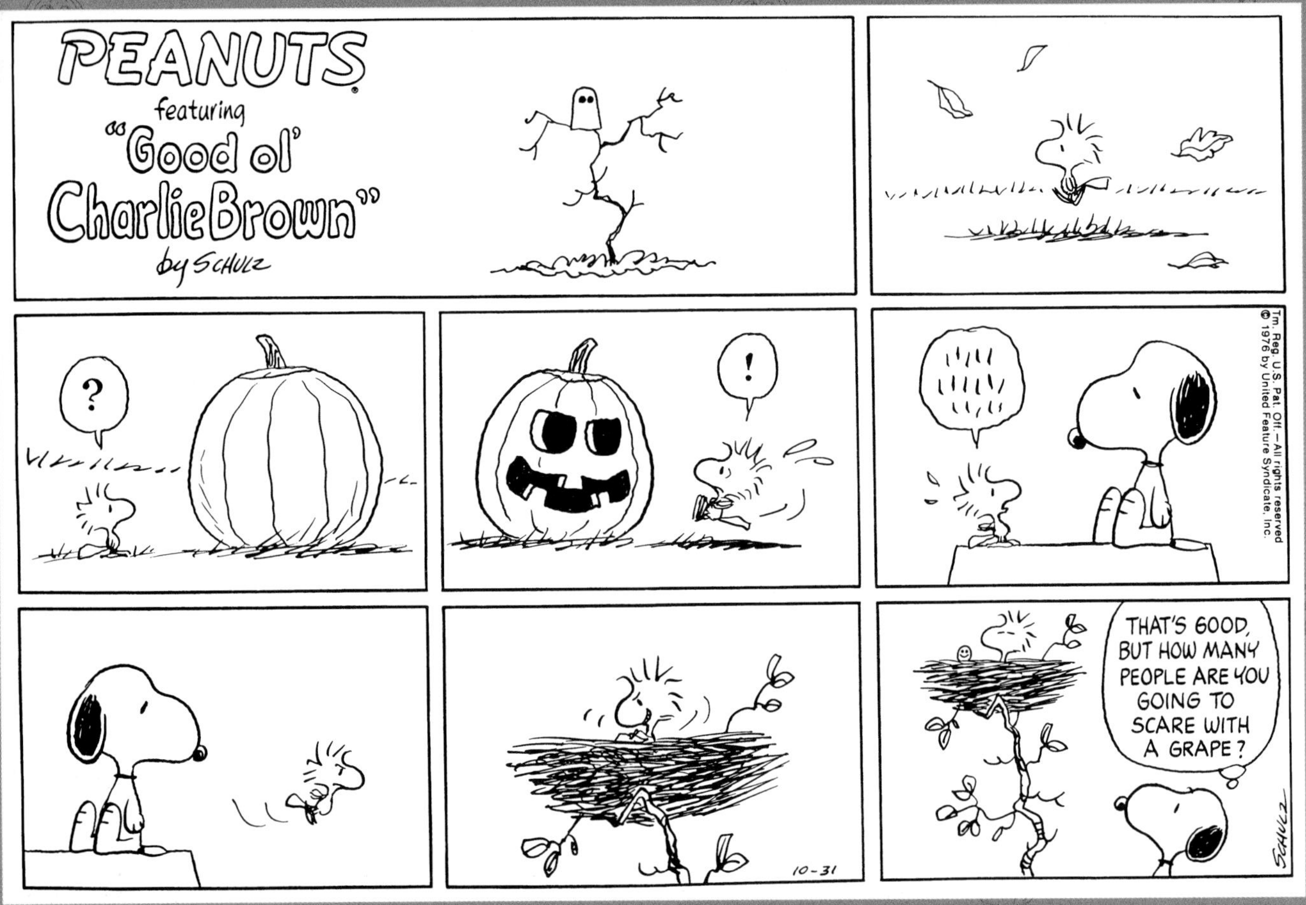
PEANUTS
featuring
"Good ol' CharlieBrown"
by SCHULZ
?
!
THAT'S GOOD, BUT HOW MANY PEOPLE ARE YOU GOING TO SCARE WITH A GRAPE?
10-31
SCHULZ

10-31-76

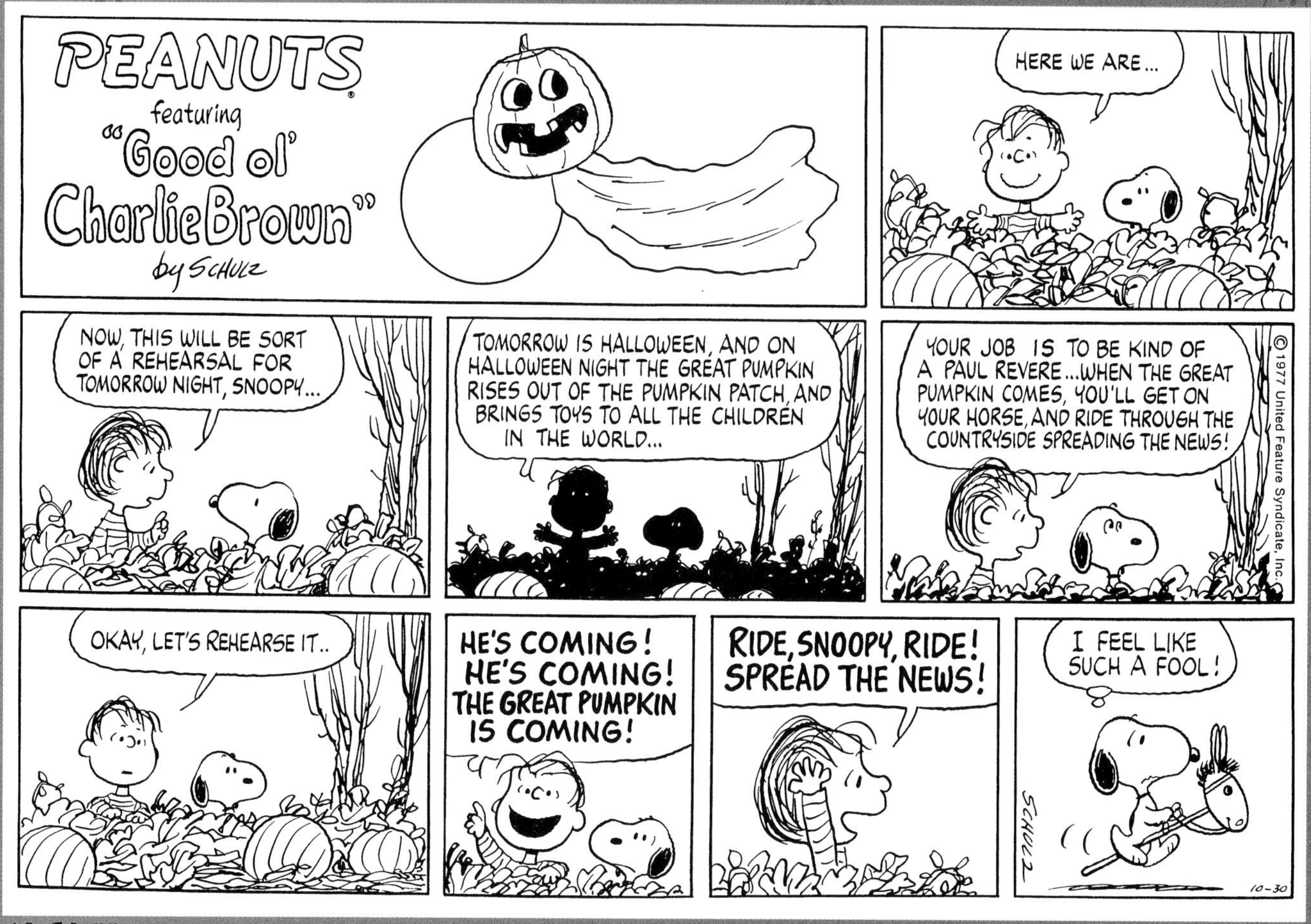
PEANUTS
featuring
"Good ol' CharlieBrown"
by SCHULZ
HERE WE ARE...
NOW, THIS WILL BE SORT OF A REHEARSAL FOR TOMORROW NIGHT, SNOOPY...
TOMORROW IS HALLOWEEN, AND ON HALLOWEEN NIGHT THE GREAT PUMPKIN RISES OUT OF THE PUMPKIN PATCH, AND BRINGS TOYS TO ALL THE CHILDREN IN THE WORLD...
YOUR JOB IS TO BE KIND OF A PAUL REVERE...WHEN THE GREAT PUMPKIN COMES, YOU'LL GET ON YOUR HORSE, AND RIDE THROUGH THE COUNTRYSIDE SPREADING THE NEWS!
© 1977 United Feature Syndicate, Inc.
OKAY, LET'S REHEARSE IT..
HE'S COMING! HE'S COMING! THE GREAT PUMPKIN IS COMING!
RIDE, SNOOPY, RIDE! SPREAD THE NEWS!
I FEEL LIKE SUCH A FOOL!
SCHULZ
10-30

10-30-77

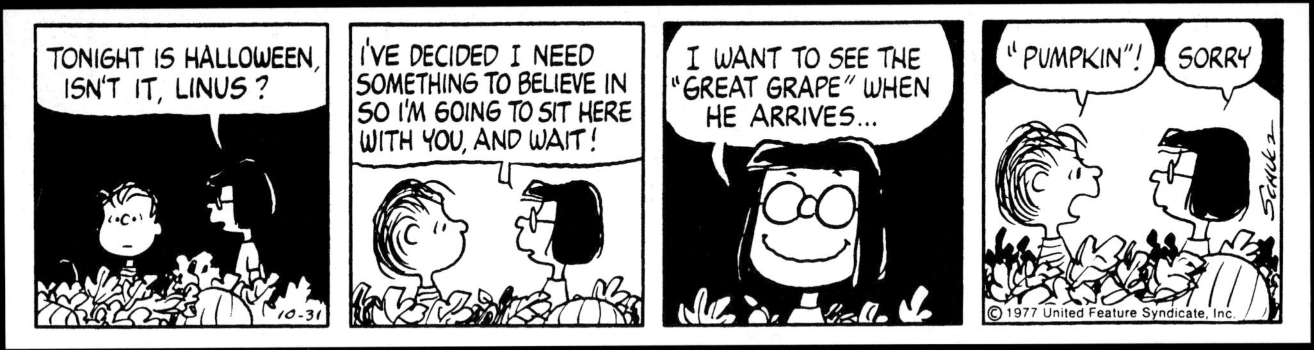
TONIGHT IS HALLOWEEN, ISN'T IT, LINUS ?
I'VE DECIDED I NEED SOMETHING TO BELIEVE IN SO I'M GOING TO SIT HERE WITH YOU, AND WAIT !
I WANT TO SEE THE "GREAT GRAPE" WHEN HE ARRIVES...
"PUMPKIN"!
SORRY
© 1977 United Feature Syndicate, Inc.

10-31-77

YOU HAVE THE LEAD IN A STAGE PLAY?
3-19
THAT'S GREAT... MAY I SEE THE PROGRAM?
HMM..."DR. BEAGLE...
... AND MR. HYDE"
SCHULZ
© 1980 United Feature Syndicate, Inc.

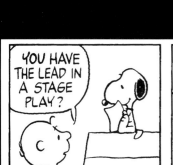

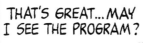

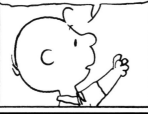

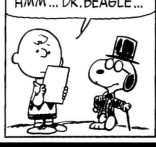

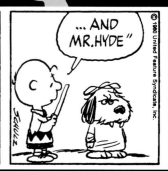

3-19-80

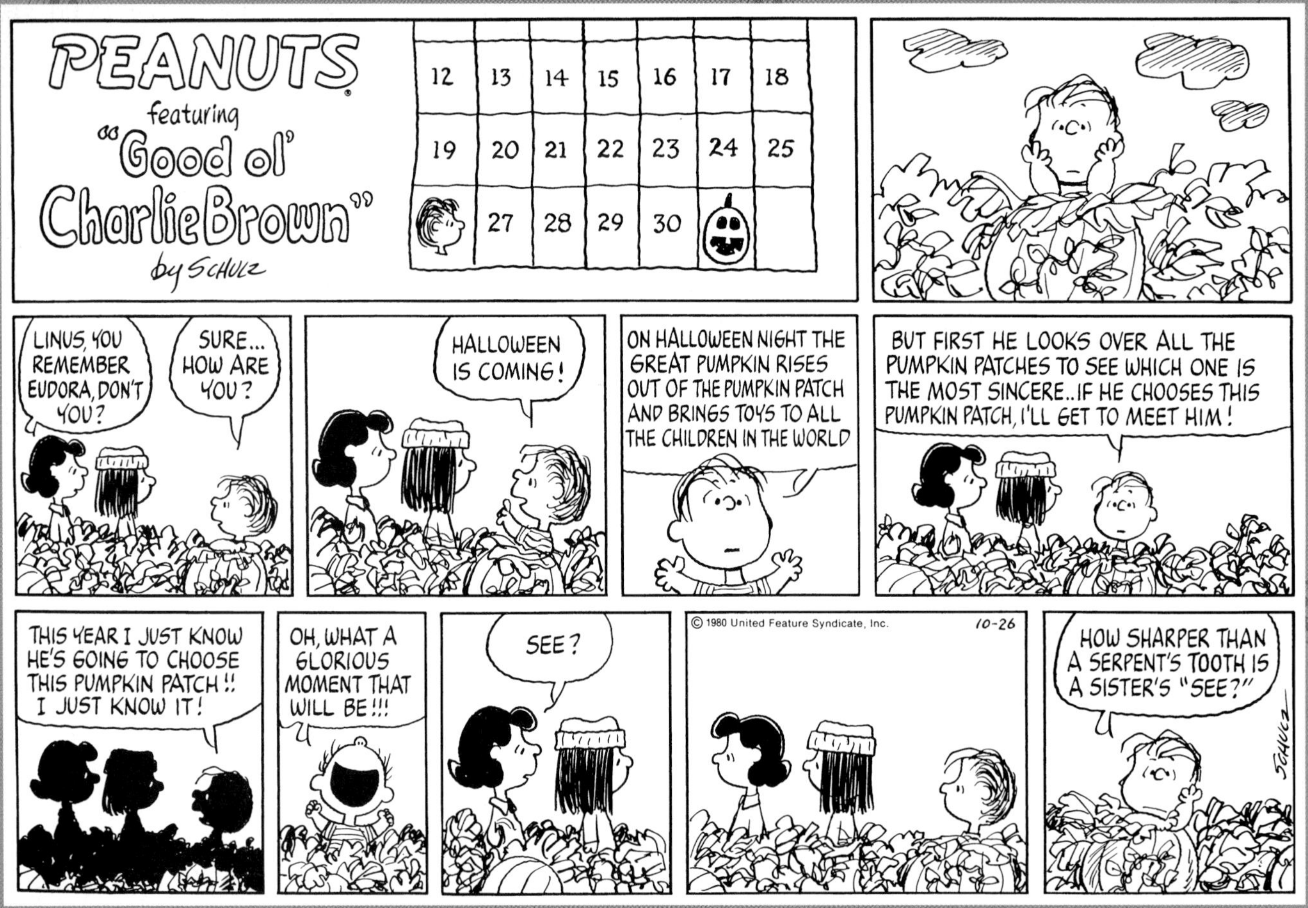
PEANUTS
featuring
"Good ol' CharlieBrown"
by SCHULZ
12 13 14 15 16 17 18
19 20 21 22 23 24 25
27 28 29 30
LINUS, YOU REMEMBER EUDORA, DON'T YOU?
SURE... HOW ARE YOU?
HALLOWEEN IS COMING!
ON HALLOWEEN NIGHT THE GREAT PUMPKIN RISES OUT OF THE PUMPKIN PATCH AND BRINGS TOYS TO ALL THE CHILDREN IN THE WORLD
BUT FIRST HE LOOKS OVER ALL THE PUMPKIN PATCHES TO SEE WHICH ONE IS THE MOST SINCERE..IF HE CHOOSES THIS PUMPKIN PATCH, I'LL GET TO MEET HIM!
THIS YEAR I JUST KNOW HE'S GOING TO CHOOSE THIS PUMPKIN PATCH!! I JUST KNOW IT!
OH, WHAT A GLORIOUS MOMENT THAT WILL BE!!!
SEE?
© 1980 United Feature Syndicate, Inc.
10-26
HOW SHARPER THAN A SERPENT'S TOOTH IS A SISTER'S "SEE?"
SCHULZ

10-26-80

ARE YOU AWARE THAT HALLOWEEN IS COMING?
ON HALLOWEEN THE "GREAT PUMPKIN" RISES OUT OF THE PUMPKIN PATCH, AND BRINGS TOYS TO ALL THE CHILDREN IN THE WORLD!
10-29
I FIND THAT HARD TO BELIEVE
MY SWEET BABBOO SAYS IT'S TRUE
HOWEVER, I'M NOT YOUR SWEET BABBOO!
© 1981 United Feature Syndicate, Inc.
SCHULZ

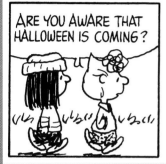

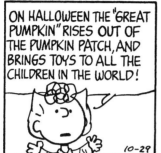

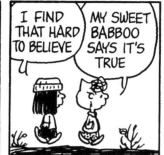

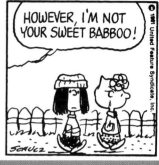

10-29-81

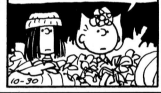

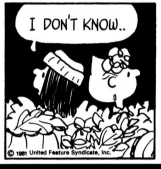

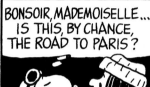

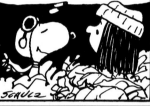

MY SWEET BABBOO SAYS IF WE SIT HERE IN THE PUMPKIN PATCH, WE MAY SEE THE "GREAT PUMPKIN"
10-30
I DON'T KNOW..
© 1981 United Feature Syndicate, Inc.
YOU CAN PROBABLY SEE A LOT OF STRANGE THINGS IN A PUMPKIN PATCH...
BONSOIR, MADEMOISELLE... IS THIS, BY CHANCE, THE ROAD TO PARIS?
SCHULZ
10-30-81

THIS IS RIDICULOUS! I'VE WASTED ALL THIS TIME SITTING HERE IN A PUMPKIN PATCH!
10-31
I TOLD YOU THERE'S NO "GREAT PUMPKIN"!
© 1981 United Feature Syndicate, Inc.
WHAT AM I GOING TO DO THE REST OF THE EVENING?
"AIMERIEZ-VOUS ALLER DANSER?" WOULD YOU LIKE TO GO DANCING?
SCHULZ

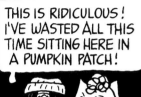

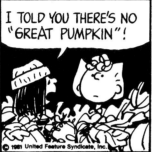

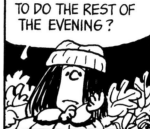

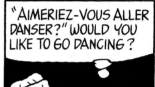

10-31-81

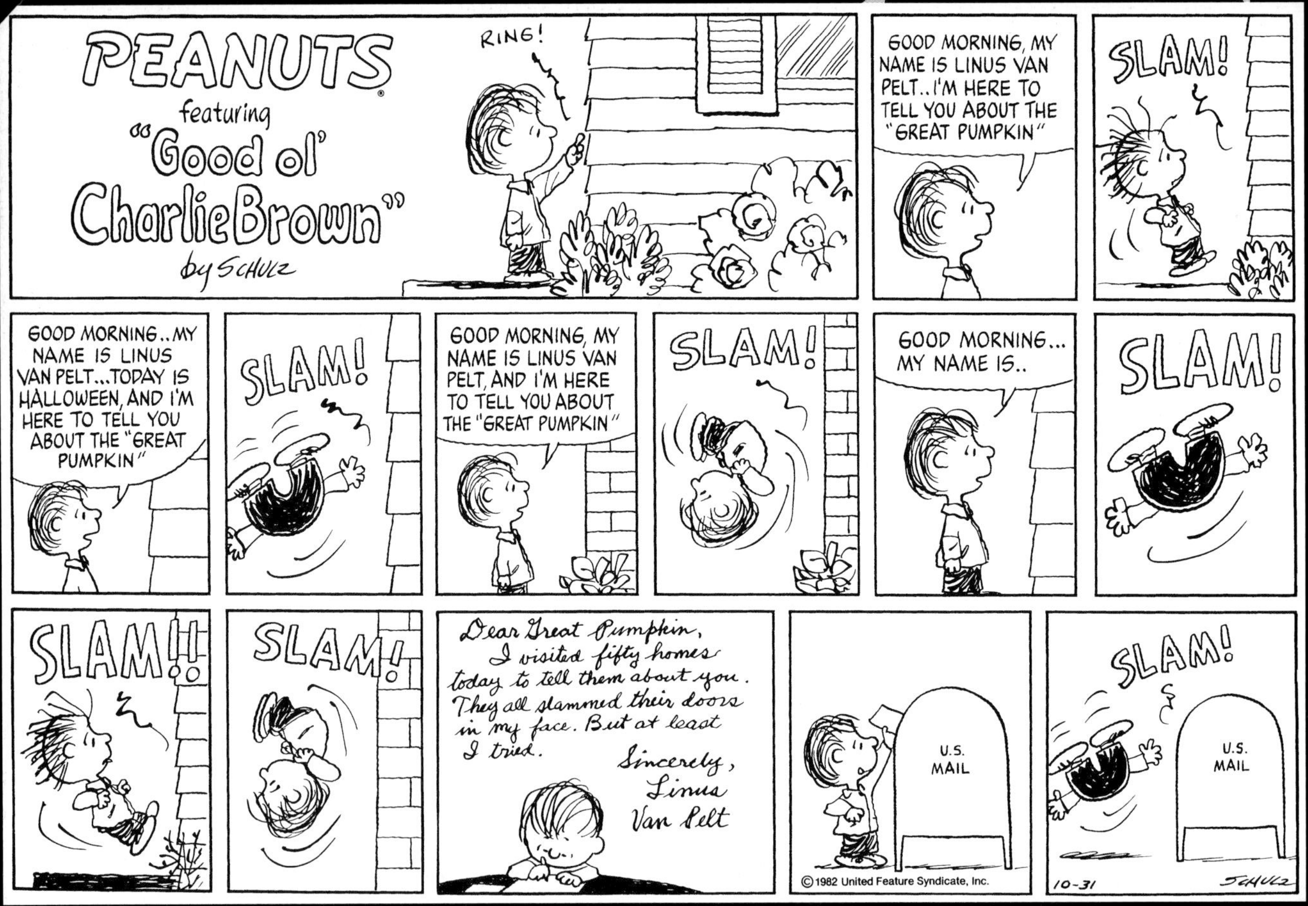
PEANUTS®
featuring
"Good ol' CharlieBrown"
by SCHULZ
RING!
GOOD MORNING, MY NAME IS LINUS VAN PELT..I'M HERE TO TELL YOU ABOUT THE "GREAT PUMPKIN"
SLAM!
GOOD MORNING..MY NAME IS LINUS VAN PELT...TODAY IS HALLOWEEN, AND I'M HERE TO TELL YOU ABOUT THE "GREAT PUMPKIN"
SLAM!
GOOD MORNING, MY NAME IS LINUS VAN PELT, AND I'M HERE TO TELL YOU ABOUT THE "GREAT PUMPKIN"
SLAM!
GOOD MORNING... MY NAME IS..
SLAM!
SLAM!!
SLAM!
Dear Great Pumpkin,
I visited fifty homes today to tell them about you. They all slammed their doors in my face. But at least I tried.
Sincerely,
Linus Van Pelt
U.S. MAIL
©1982 United Feature Syndicate, Inc.
SLAM!
U.S. MAIL
10-31
SCHULZ

10-31-82

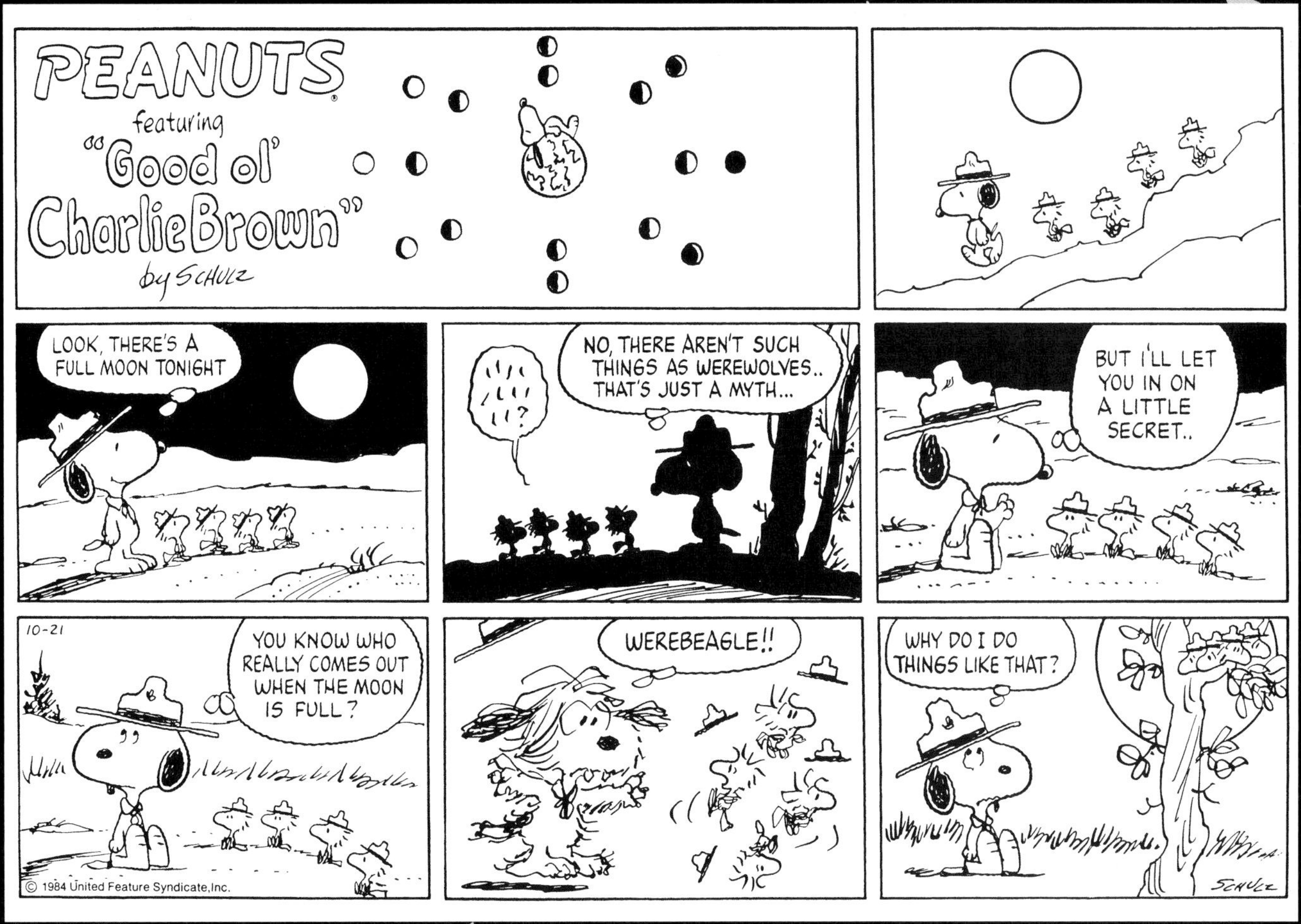
PEANUTS
featuring
"Good ol' Charlie Brown"
by SCHULZ
LOOK, THERE'S A FULL MOON TONIGHT
NO, THERE AREN'T SUCH THINGS AS WEREWOLVES.. THAT'S JUST A MYTH...
BUT I'LL LET YOU IN ON A LITTLE SECRET..
10-21
YOU KNOW WHO REALLY COMES OUT WHEN THE MOON IS FULL?
© 1984 United Feature Syndicate, Inc.
WEREBEAGLE!!
WHY DO I DO THINGS LIKE THAT?
SCHULZ

10-21-84

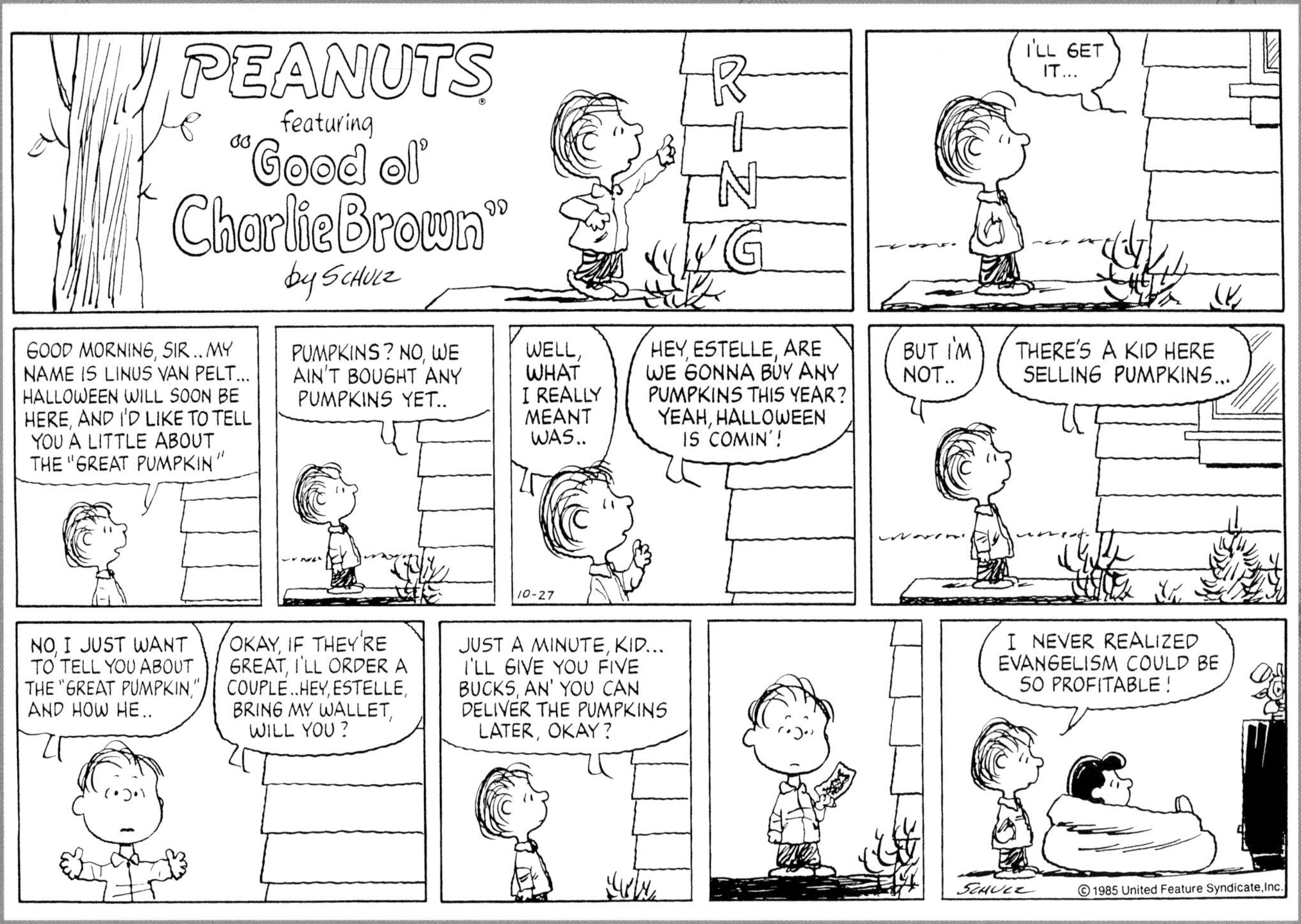
PEANUTS
featuring
"Good ol' Charlie Brown"
by SCHULZ
RING
I'LL GET IT...
GOOD MORNING, SIR.. MY NAME IS LINUS VAN PELT... HALLOWEEN WILL SOON BE HERE, AND I'D LIKE TO TELL YOU A LITTLE ABOUT THE "GREAT PUMPKIN"
PUMPKINS? NO, WE AIN'T BOUGHT ANY PUMPKINS YET..
WELL, WHAT I REALLY MEANT WAS..
HEY, ESTELLE, ARE WE GONNA BUY ANY PUMPKINS THIS YEAR? YEAH, HALLOWEEN IS COMIN'!
10-27
BUT I'M NOT..
THERE'S A KID HERE SELLING PUMPKINS...
NO, I JUST WANT TO TELL YOU ABOUT THE "GREAT PUMPKIN," AND HOW HE..
OKAY, IF THEY'RE GREAT, I'LL ORDER A COUPLE..HEY, ESTELLE, BRING MY WALLET, WILL YOU?
JUST A MINUTE, KID... I'LL GIVE YOU FIVE BUCKS, AN' YOU CAN DELIVER THE PUMPKINS LATER, OKAY?
I NEVER REALIZED EVANGELISM COULD BE SO PROFITABLE!
SCHULZ
© 1985 United Feature Syndicate, Inc.

10-27-85

10-31
© 1985 United Feature Syndicate, Inc.
RING!
I FORGOT THE WORDS!
SCHULZ

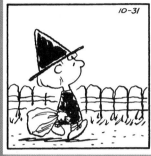

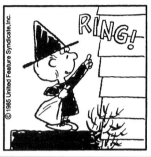

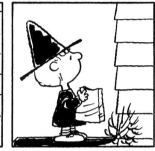

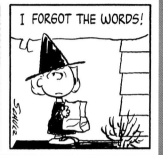

10-31-85

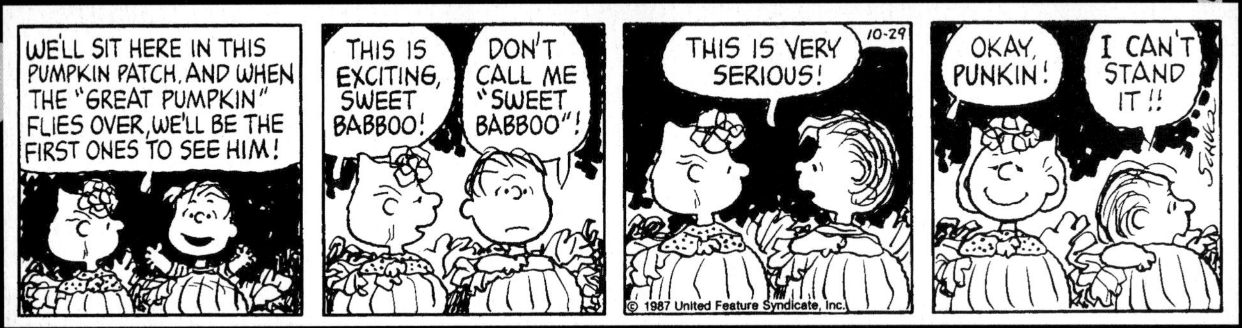
WE'LL SIT HERE IN THIS PUMPKIN PATCH, AND WHEN THE "GREAT PUMPKIN" FLIES OVER, WE'LL BE THE FIRST ONES TO SEE HIM!
THIS IS EXCITING, SWEET BABBOO!
DON'T CALL ME "SWEET BABBOO"!
10-29
THIS IS VERY SERIOUS!
© 1987 United Feature Syndicate, Inc.
OKAY, PUNKIN!
I CAN'T STAND IT!!
SCHULZ

10-29-87

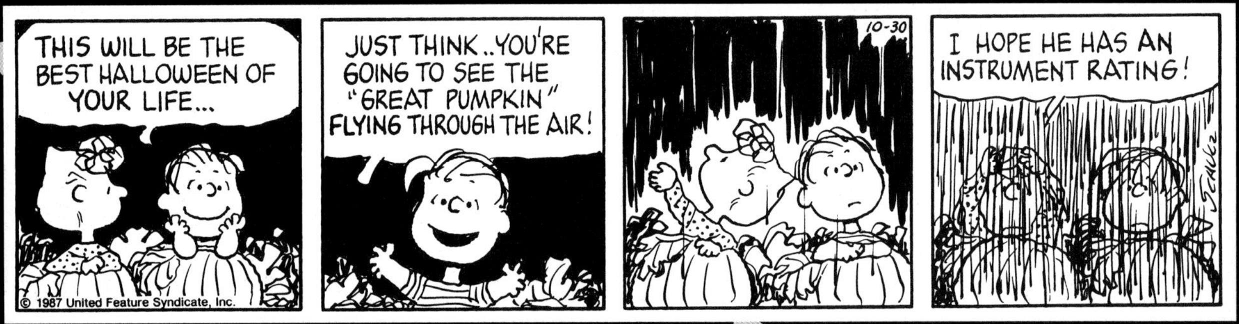
THIS WILL BE THE BEST HALLOWEEN OF YOUR LIFE...
© 1987 United Feature Syndicate, Inc.
JUST THINK..YOU'RE GOING TO SEE THE "GREAT PUMPKIN" FLYING THROUGH THE AIR!
10-30
I HOPE HE HAS AN INSTRUMENT RATING!
SCHULZ

10-30-87

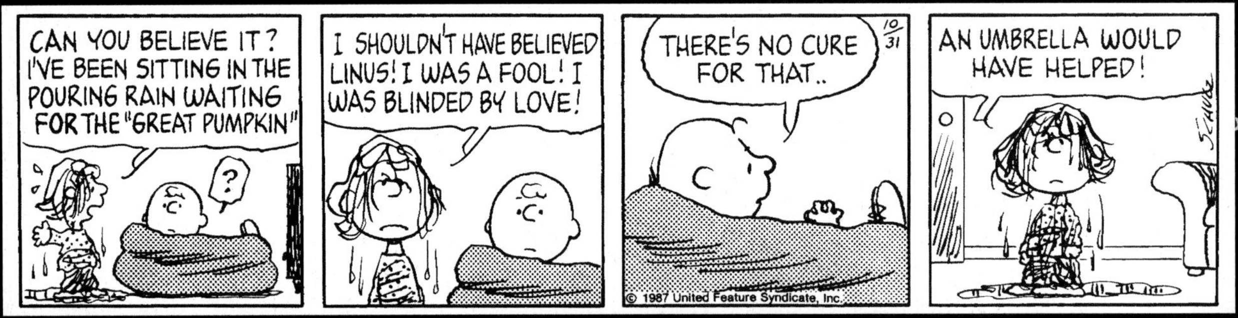
CAN YOU BELIEVE IT? I'VE BEEN SITTING IN THE POURING RAIN WAITING FOR THE "GREAT PUMPKIN"
?
I SHOULDN'T HAVE BELIEVED LINUS! I WAS A FOOL! I WAS BLINDED BY LOVE!
10/31
THERE'S NO CURE FOR THAT..
© 1987 United Feature Syndicate, Inc.
AN UMBRELLA WOULD HAVE HELPED!
SCHULZ

10-31-87

TONIGHT IS HALLOWEEN..HOW COME YOU'RE NOT SITTING OUT IN A PUMPKIN PATCH WAITING FOR THE GREAT PUMPKIN, AND MAKING A TOTAL, COMPLETE AND ABSOLUTE FOOL OF YOURSELF?
YOU HAVE A NICE WAY OF WORDING THINGS..
THANK YOU.. I WORK THEM OUT ON LITTLE SLIPS OF PAPER BEFOREHAND..
10-31
© 1988 United Feature Syndicate, Inc.

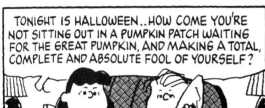

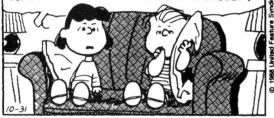

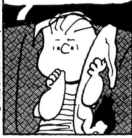

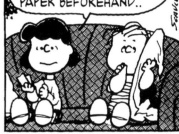

10-31-88

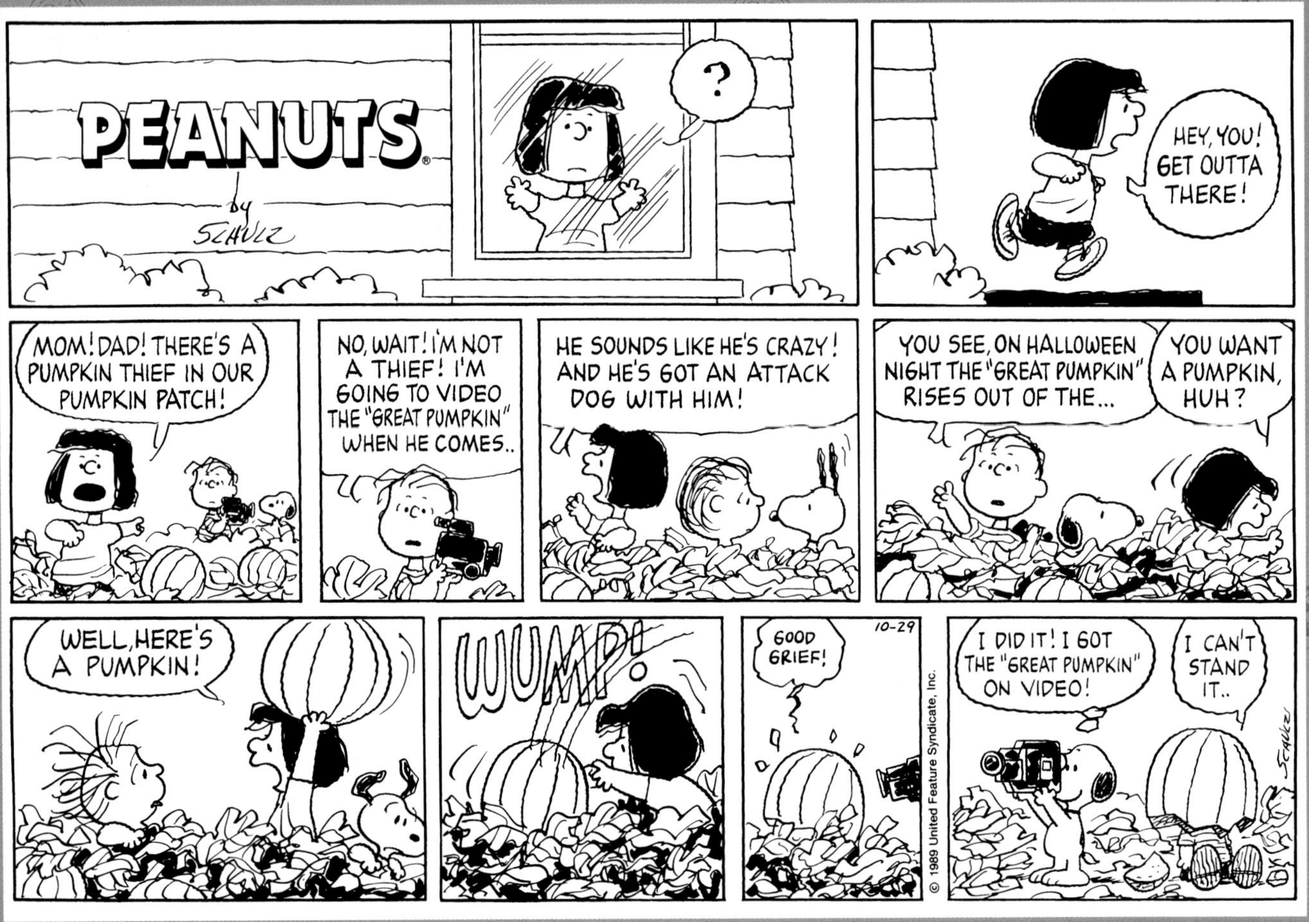
PEANUTS
by SCHULZ
?
HEY, YOU! GET OUTTA THERE!
MOM! DAD! THERE'S A PUMPKIN THIEF IN OUR PUMPKIN PATCH!
NO, WAIT! I'M NOT A THIEF! I'M GOING TO VIDEO THE "GREAT PUMPKIN" WHEN HE COMES..
HE SOUNDS LIKE HE'S CRAZY! AND HE'S GOT AN ATTACK DOG WITH HIM!
YOU SEE, ON HALLOWEEN NIGHT THE "GREAT PUMPKIN" RISES OUT OF THE...
YOU WANT A PUMPKIN, HUH?
WELL, HERE'S A PUMPKIN!
WUMP!
GOOD GRIEF!
10-29
© 1989 United Feature Syndicate, Inc.
I DID IT! I GOT THE "GREAT PUMPKIN" ON VIDEO!
I CAN'T STAND IT..
SCHULZ

10-29-89

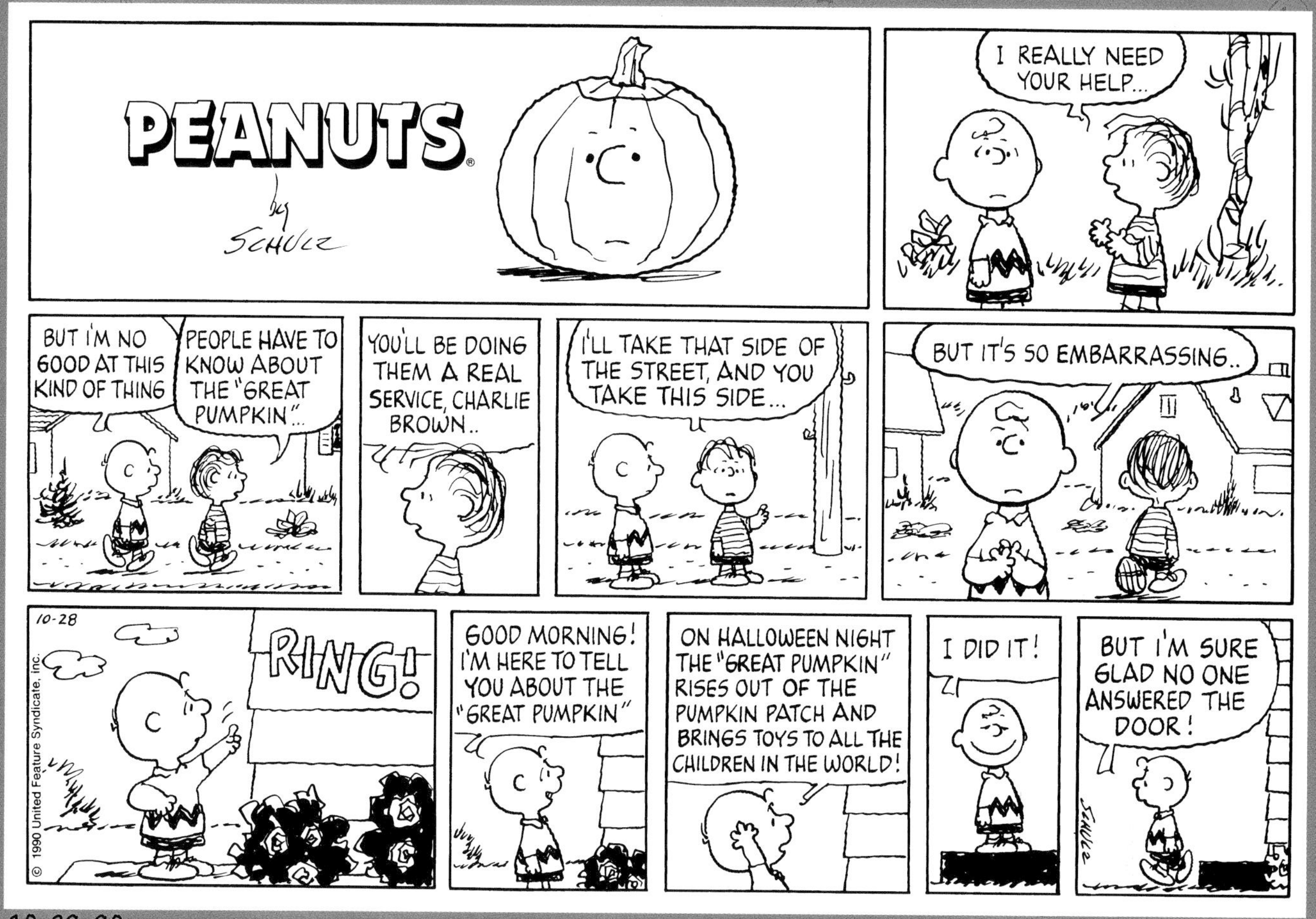
PEANUTS
by SCHULZ
I REALLY NEED YOUR HELP...
BUT I'M NO GOOD AT THIS KIND OF THING
PEOPLE HAVE TO KNOW ABOUT THE "GREAT PUMPKIN"...
YOU'LL BE DOING THEM A REAL SERVICE, CHARLIE BROWN..
I'LL TAKE THAT SIDE OF THE STREET, AND YOU TAKE THIS SIDE...
BUT IT'S SO EMBARRASSING..
10-28
© 1990 United Feature Syndicate, Inc.
RING!
GOOD MORNING! I'M HERE TO TELL YOU ABOUT THE "GREAT PUMPKIN"
ON HALLOWEEN NIGHT THE "GREAT PUMPKIN" RISES OUT OF THE PUMPKIN PATCH AND BRINGS TOYS TO ALL THE CHILDREN IN THE WORLD!
I DID IT!
BUT I'M SURE GLAD NO ONE ANSWERED THE DOOR!
SCHULZ

10-29-90

It was a dark and stormy night.
Suddenly, out of the mist a spooky figure appeared.
© 1991 United Feature Syndicate, Inc.
7-8
How spooky was he?
Spoooooooky!
SCHULZ

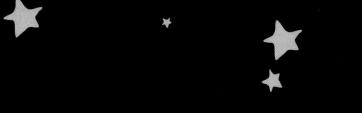

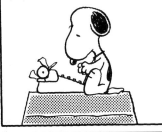

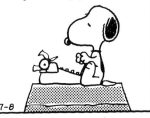

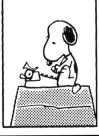

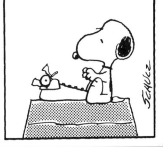

7-8-91

HALLOWEEN IS OVER, AND THE "GREAT PUMPKIN" DIDN'T SHOW UP AGAIN, DID HE ?
NO, SHE DIDN'T, DID SHE ?
11-1
NEVER EVEN OCCURRED TO YOU, DID IT ?
SCHULZ
© 1991 United Feature Syndicate, Inc.

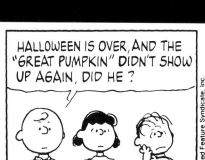

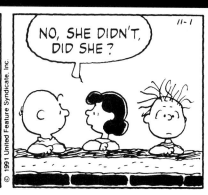

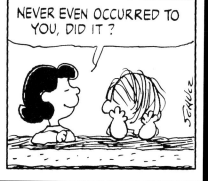

11-1-91

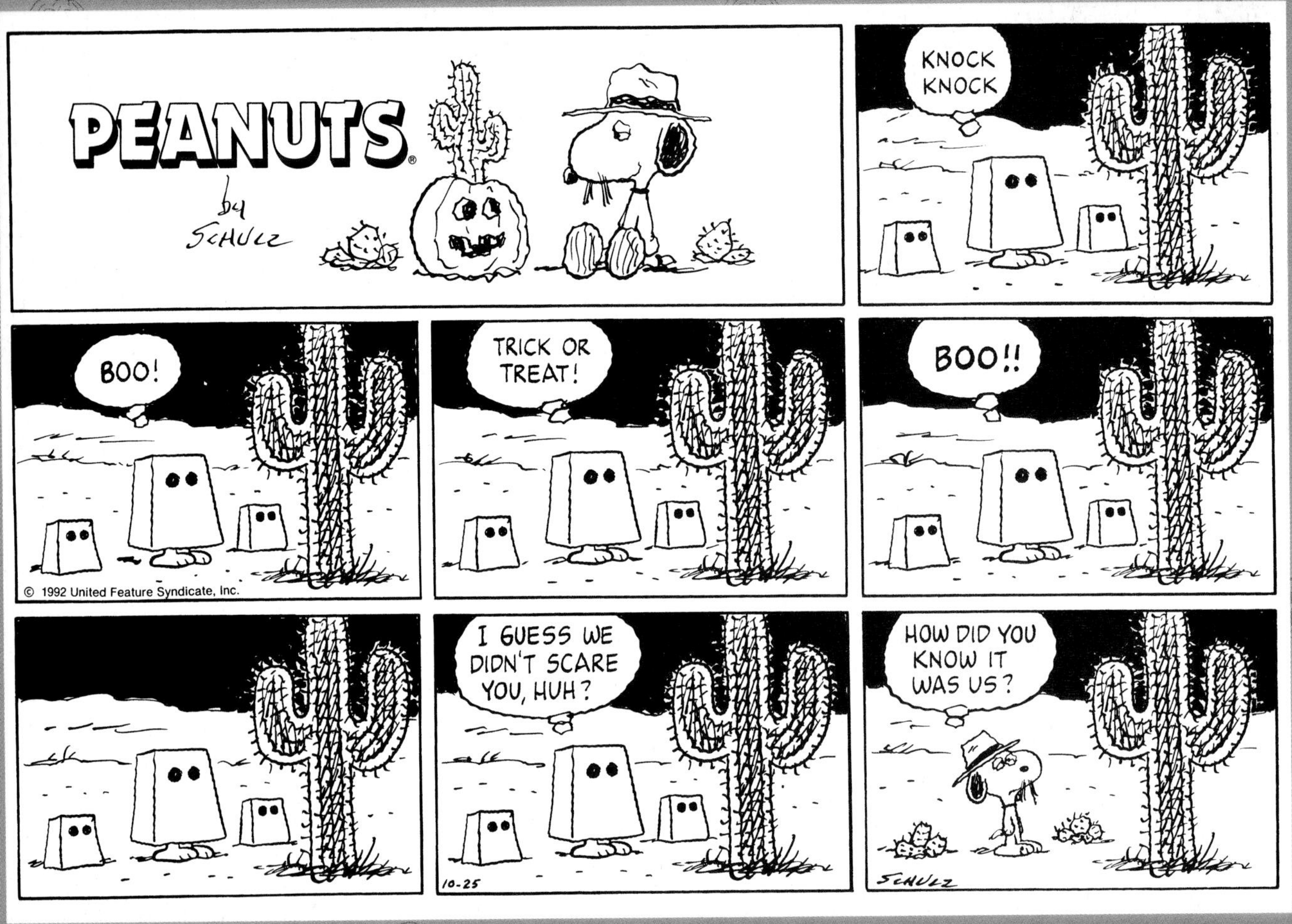
PEANUTS
by SCHULZ
KNOCK KNOCK
BOO!
© 1992 United Feature Syndicate, Inc.
TRICK OR TREAT!
BOO!!
I GUESS WE DIDN'T SCARE YOU, HUH?
10-25
HOW DID YOU KNOW IT WAS US?
SCHULZ

10-25-92

HALLOWEEN IS ALMOST HERE, ISN'T IT?
I SUPPOSE YOU'LL BE WAITING FOR THE "GREAT GRAPE" TO COME AGAIN, HUH?
PUMPKIN!
10-26
© 1992 United Feature Syndicate, Inc.
OH, SORRY..I GUESS IT WOULD BE HARD TO CARVE A SCARY FACE ON A GRAPE, WOULDN'T IT?
I CAN'T STAND IT!
SCHULZ

10-26-92

I LOVE HALLOWEEN.. WITH THESE BINOCULARS WE'LL BE ABLE TO SEE THE "GREAT PUMPKIN" COME FLYING IN!
I CAN SEE THE BIG DIPPER..
I HOPE YOU'RE NOT WASTING YOUR TIME LOOKING AT THE BIG DIPPER..
I CAN SEE THE CRATERS ON THE MOON..
© 1994 United Feature Syndicate, Inc.
10/31
I HOPE YOU'RE NOT WASTING YOUR TIME LOOKING AT THE MOON..
I CAN SEE A STUPID KID SITTING IN A PUMPKIN PATCH..
SCHULZ

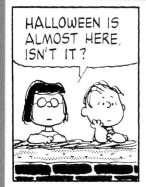

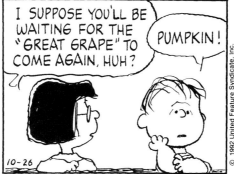

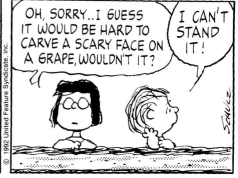

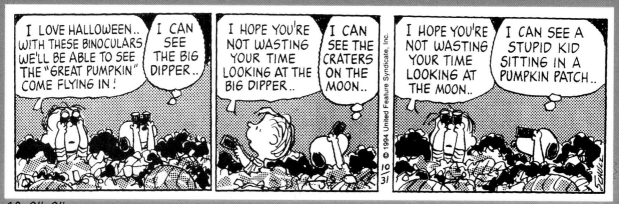

10-94-94

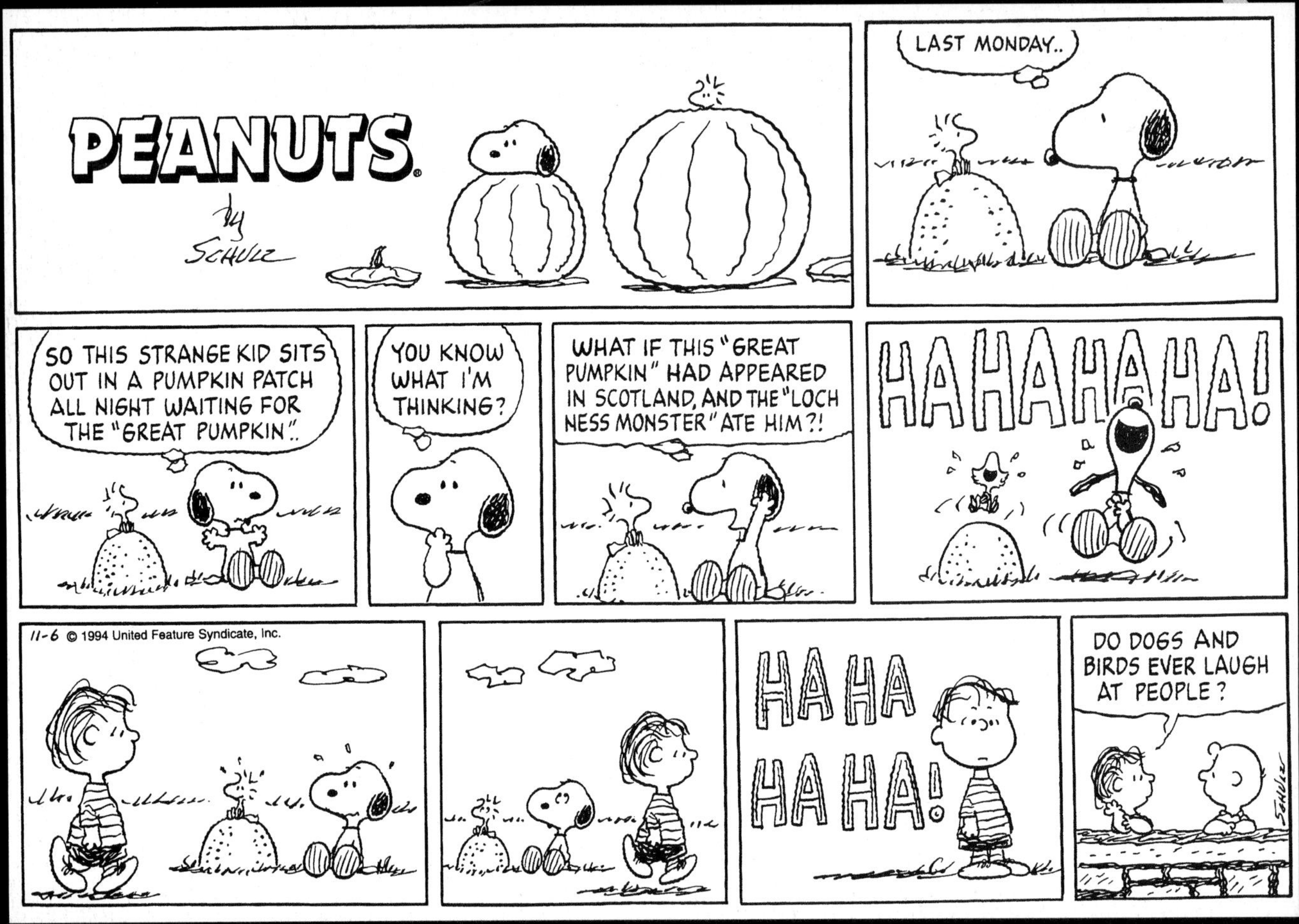
PEANUTS
by SCHULZ
LAST MONDAY..
SO THIS STRANGE KID SITS OUT IN A PUMPKIN PATCH ALL NIGHT WAITING FOR THE "GREAT PUMPKIN".
YOU KNOW WHAT I'M THINKING?
WHAT IF THIS "GREAT PUMPKIN" HAD APPEARED IN SCOTLAND, AND THE "LOCH NESS MONSTER" ATE HIM?!
HAHAHAHAHA!
11-6 © 1994 United Feature Syndicate, Inc.
HA HA HA HA!
DO DOGS AND BIRDS EVER LAUGH AT PEOPLE?
SCHULZ

11-6-94

SEE THAT HOUSE WE'RE COMING TO? THEY SAY IT'S A HAUNTED HOUSE..
I DON'T BELIEVE IN HAUNTED HOUSES..
3-13
BUT I'LL WALK ON THIS SIDE OF YOU..
SCHULZ
© 1995 United Feature Syndicate, Inc.

3-13-95

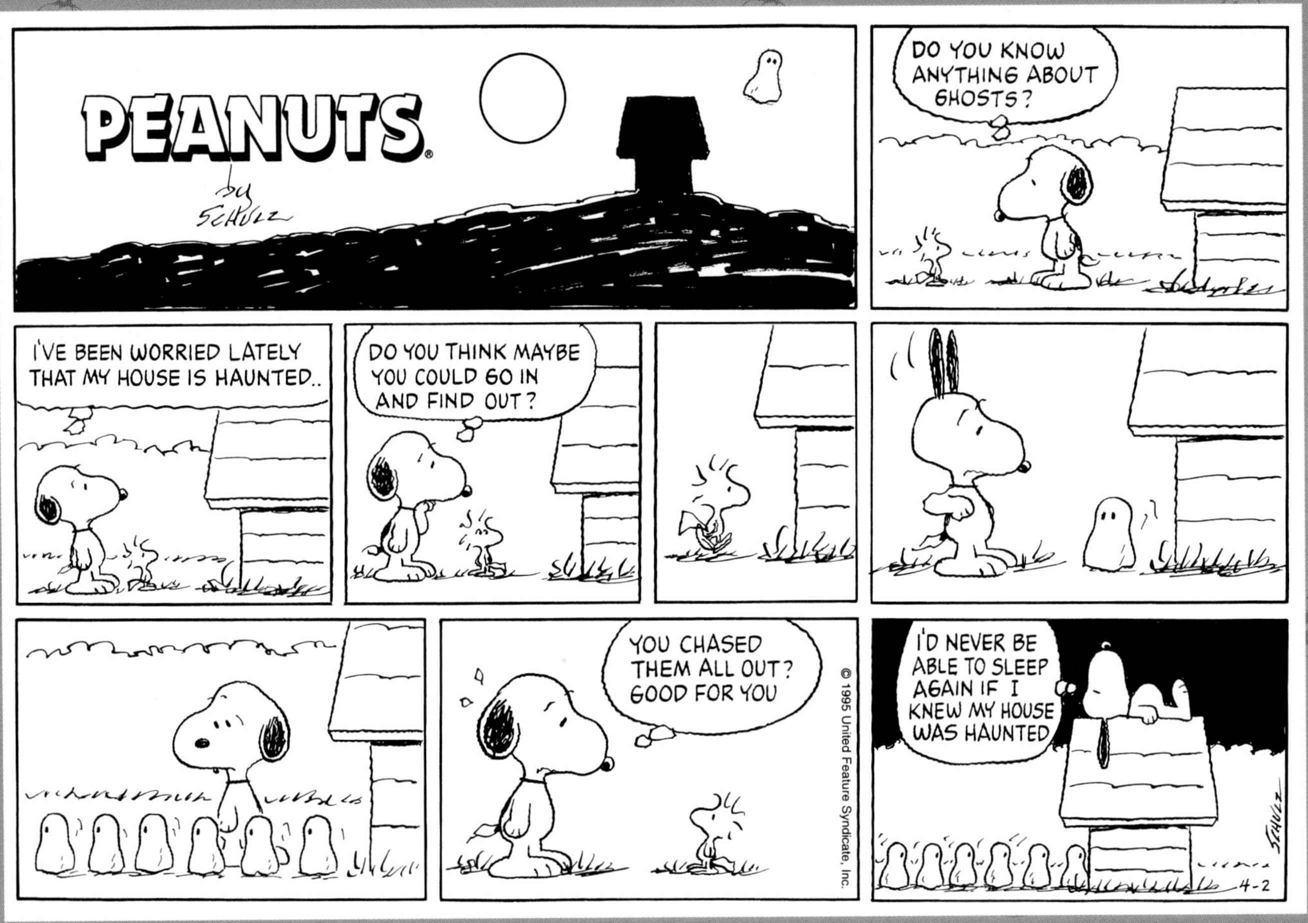
PEANUTS
by SCHULZ
DO YOU KNOW ANYTHING ABOUT GHOSTS?
I'VE BEEN WORRIED LATELY THAT MY HOUSE IS HAUNTED..
DO YOU THINK MAYBE YOU COULD GO IN AND FIND OUT?
YOU CHASED THEM ALL OUT? GOOD FOR YOU
© 1995 United Feature Syndicate, Inc.
I'D NEVER BE ABLE TO SLEEP AGAIN IF I KNEW MY HOUSE WAS HAUNTED
SCHULZ
4-2

4-2-95

Handprint Ghosts

Remember those handprint Thanksgiving turkeys we made in grammar school—our palm for the body, thumb for its head, and fingers for its feathers? These handprint ghosts turn that turkey on its head! In this fast and fun project, the body of the turkey becomes the head of the ghost, and the feathers and head form its flowing bottom. The handprint ghosts make fun place cards or name tags, as well as an eerily cute Halloween greeting.

Trace your hand on the sheet of paper and turn it upside down. Draw a half circle at the top to join the two lines where your wrist was. Draw eyes, or glue wiggle eyes, on the head, and draw a big O for the mouth. Cut out the ghost. If you like, write a note on the back.

For each ghost you will need:

• white construction paper
• black magic marker or wiggle eyes
• craft glue (if using wiggle eyes)

© 1996 United Feature Syndicate, Inc.
10-28
ON HALLOWEEN NIGHT, THE "GREAT PUMPKIN" RISES OUT OF THE PUMPKIN PATCH, AND..
YOU'RE JUST TRYING TO MESS WITH MY MIND, AREN'T YOU?
SCHULZ

10-28-96

ARE YOU THE "GREAT PUMPKIN"?
NO, I'M YOUR KID BROTHER WITH A SHEET OVER MY HEAD..
© 1996 United Feature Syndicate, Inc.
I FORGOT TO CUT OUT THE EYE HOLES SO I HAVE NO IDEA WHERE I'M GOING..
10-31
SCHULZ

10-31-96

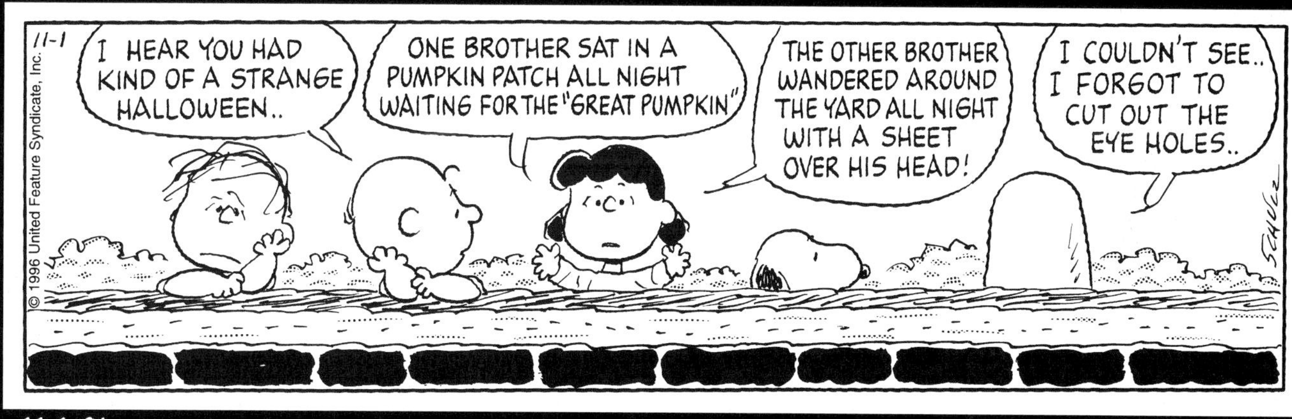
11-1
© 1996 United Feature Syndicate, Inc.
I HEAR YOU HAD KIND OF A STRANGE HALLOWEEN..
ONE BROTHER SAT IN A PUMPKIN PATCH ALL NIGHT WAITING FOR THE "GREAT PUMPKIN"
THE OTHER BROTHER WANDERED AROUND THE YARD ALL NIGHT WITH A SHEET OVER HIS HEAD!
I COULDN'T SEE.. I FORGOT TO CUT OUT THE EYE HOLES..
SCHULZ

11-1-96

9-10
DIDN'T SCARE ME A BIT..
BIRDS CAN'T SAY, "BOO!"
SCHULZ
www.unitedmedia.com
© 1997 United Feature Syndicate, Inc.

9-10-97

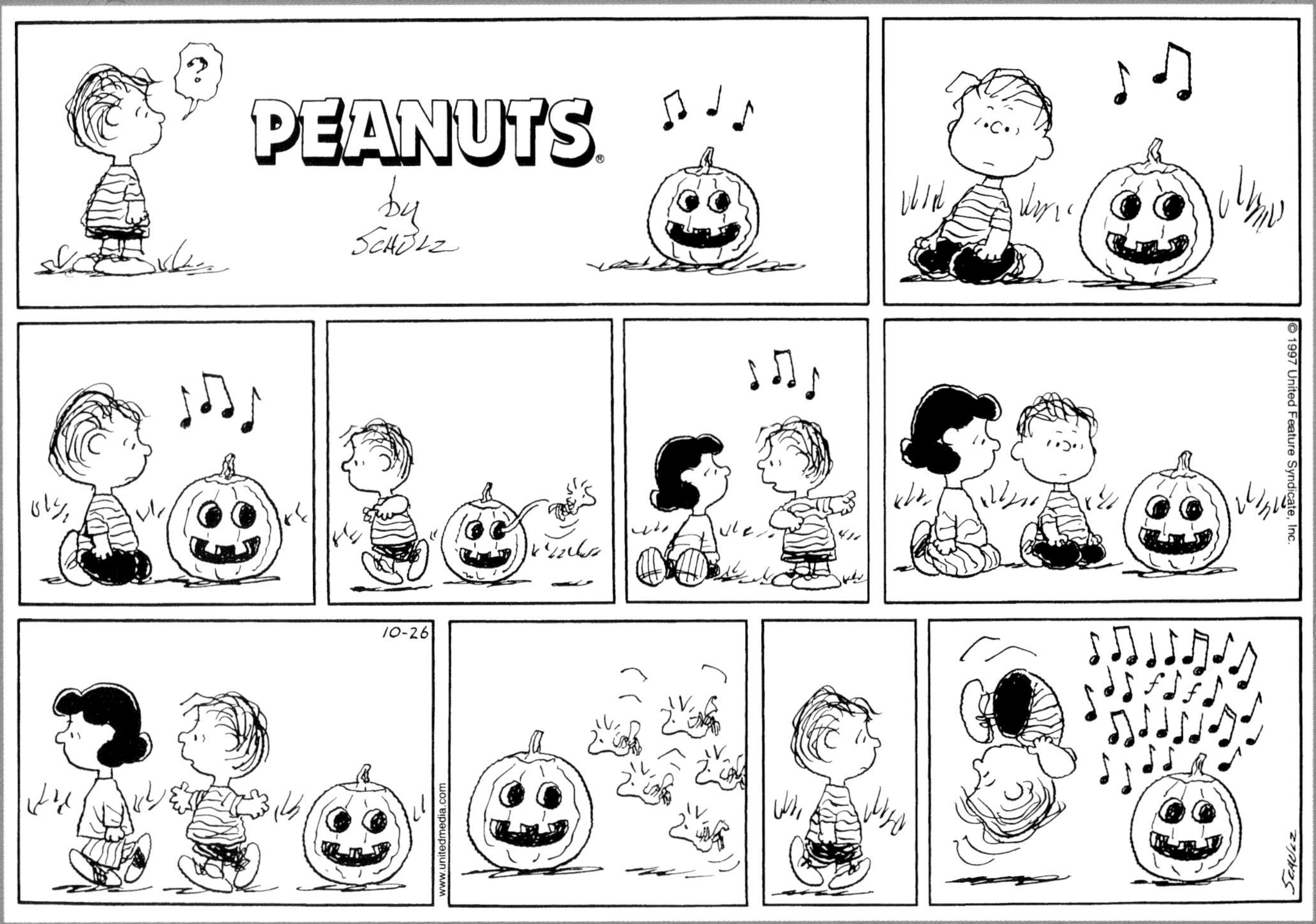
?
PEANUTS
by SCHULZ
© 1997 United Feature Syndicate, Inc.
10-26
www.unitedmedia.com
SCHULZ

10-26-97

Party Snack Mix

- 4 cups bite-size crispy corn squares cereal

- 2 cups bite-size crispy wheat squares cereal

- 2 cups pretzel sticks

- 2 cups Spanish peanuts or mixed nuts

- ½ cup butter, melted

- 1 tablespoon Worcestershire sauce

- ⅛ teaspoon hot pepper sauce

- 1 teaspoon salt

- ¼ teaspoon garlic powder

Heat oven to 325°F. In a large bowl, combine cereals, pretzel sticks, and peanuts.

In a small bowl, combine butter, Worcestershire sauce, hot pepper sauce, salt, and garlic powder; mix well. Pour seasoning mixture over cereal mixture; toss to coat. Spread in ungreased 15 x 10 x 1-inch baking pan.

Bake at 325°F for 25 to 30 minutes or until lightly toasted, stirring occasionally.

Makes 12 cups.

Maple Cider Punch

Whip up a batch of citrusy, sparkly punch for sipping while carving jack-o'-lanterns. Make a toast to the fun and frolic of Halloween. Kids can help measure and stir the ingredients.

Pour the orange juice into a small saucepan and stir in the maple syrup. Place over medium heat and bring almost to a boil. Remove from heat, stir once or twice, and let cool to room temperature. (Or combine the orange juice and maple syrup in a microwave-safe bowl and microwave on high for 3 minutes.)

Pour the apple cider into a pitcher and add the cooled orange juice and the ginger ale. Mix well. Serve over ice.

Makes 6 servings.

- 1 cup orange juice
- 3 tablespoons maple syrup
- 4 cups apple cider, chilled
- 1 cup ginger ale, chilled
- ice cubes

SO WE'LL GO FROM HOUSE TO HOUSE "TRICK OR TREATING," AND PEOPLE WILL GIVE US THINGS..
LIKE MAYBE A BICYCLE?
NO, NOT A BICYCLE.. MAYBE AN ORANGE OR A COOKIE..
A BICYCLE WOULD BE NICE..
YOU HAVE TO TAKE WHATEVER THEY GIVE YOU..
HOW DID I GET INVOLVED IN SOMETHING LIKE THIS?
www.snoopy.com
© 1998 United Feature Syndicate, Inc.
SCHULZ
10/28

10-28-98

HERE'S THE BAG YOU'LL USE TO CARRY ALL THE THINGS PEOPLE WILL GIVE YOU WHEN WE GO "TRICK OR TREATING" ON HALLOWEEN NIGHT
www.snoopy.com
WHAT IF SOMEBODY GIVES ME A BICYCLE?
NOBODY'S GOING TO GIVE YOU A BICYCLE..
10-29
© 1998 United Feature Syndicate, Inc.
I'LL JUST SAY, "THANK YOU..DON'T PUT IT IN THE BAG..I'LL RIDE IT HOME!"
SCHULZ

10-29-98

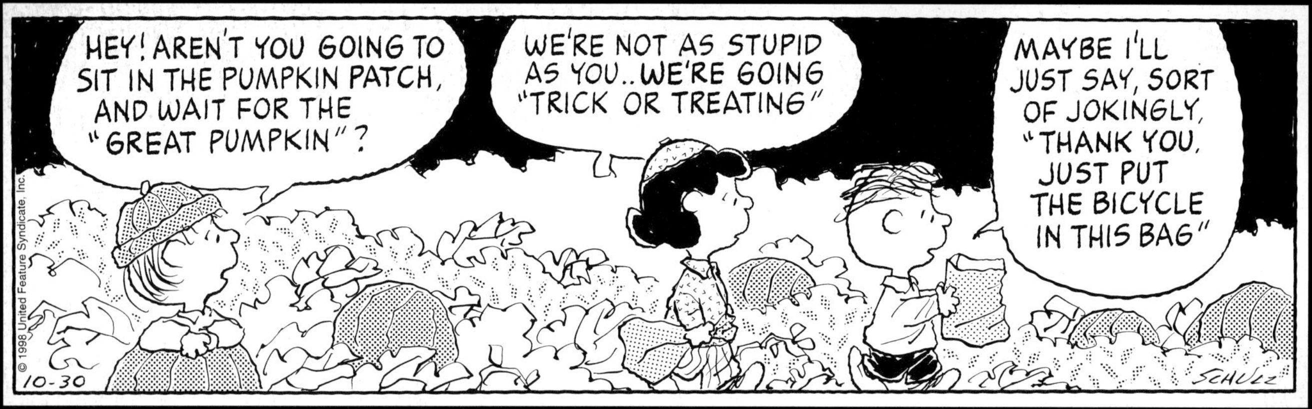
HEY! AREN'T YOU GOING TO SIT IN THE PUMPKIN PATCH, AND WAIT FOR THE "GREAT PUMPKIN"?
WE'RE NOT AS STUPID AS YOU..WE'RE GOING "TRICK OR TREATING"
MAYBE I'LL JUST SAY, SORT OF JOKINGLY, "THANK YOU, JUST PUT THE BICYCLE IN THIS BAG"
© 1998 United Feature Syndicate, Inc.
10-30
SCHULZ

10-30-98

FOR "TRICK OR TREATS" I GOT TWELVE CANDY BARS, FOURTEEN COOKIES, AND THREE TUBES OF TOOTHPASTE
www.snoopy.com
11-2
© 1998 United Feature Syndicate, Inc.
I DIDN'T GET A BICYCLE..
SCHULZ

11-2-98

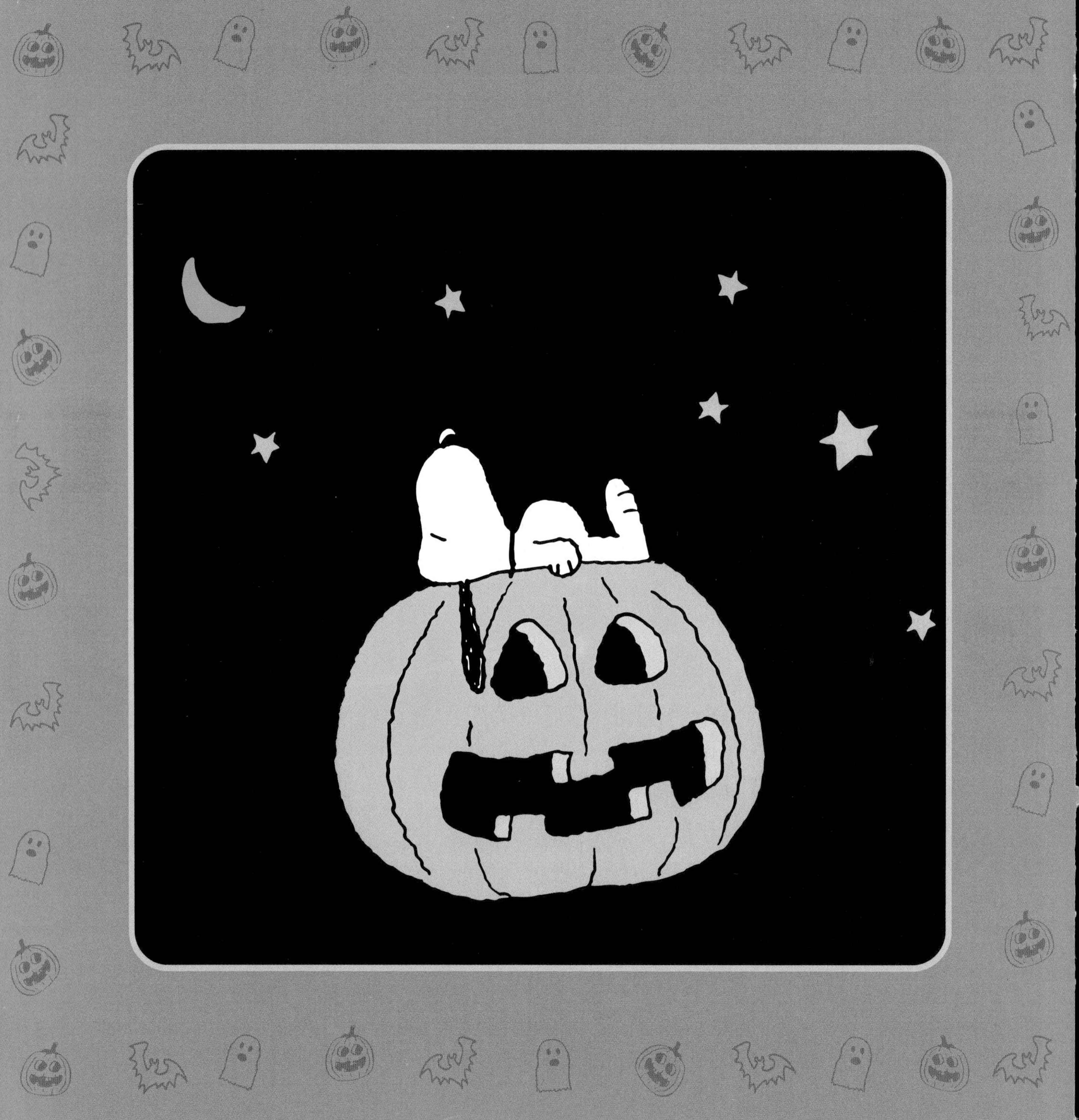